ONLY APPARENTLY REAL

ONLY APPARENTLY REAL

PAUL WILLIAMS

this book is dedicated to the memory of
Dorothy Hudner and Joseph Edgar Dick

Cover painting by Kent Bellows

2nd printing, July 1999

ISBN 0-934558-31-0
Library of Congress catalog card number:
85-23036

available from:

Entwhistle Books
Box 232517
Encinitas CA 92023

and from: www.paulwilliams.com

or: 760-753-1815

for a catalog of available back issues of the *Philip K. Dick Society Newsletter*, write to:
PKDS, Box 232517 Encinitas CA 92023
or email Paul@cdaddy.com

CONTENTS

ACKNOWLEDGMENTS

I would like to thank Jann Wenner, who originally gave me the assignment to do a profile of Philip K. Dick for *Rolling Stone,* and Paul Scanlon, my editor at *Rolling Stone,* who was extremely supportive. My thanks also to Joe Eszterhas, Sarah Lazin, Abby Bard, Greg Scott, and Kent Bellows, for their help and participation in the project. My thanks also to those who helped me research and write that 1974 profile, including Henry Ludmer, Norman Spinrad, Susan Ann Protter, John Douglas, Sachiko Williams, Donald A. Wollheim, Grania Davis, Loren Cavit, Tom Schmidt, Ted White, Theodore Sturgeon, Jean-Pierre Gorin, William Wolfson, Carol and Terry Carr, Avram Davidson, Captain Teague, Linda Herman and the staff at the Special Collections Library of California State University at Fullerton, and very special thanks to Tessa B. Dick for her hospitality, participation, and inspiration, to Christopher Dick for keeping his dad in a good mood, and most of all to Philip K. Dick, for talking, writing, making me laugh, and for being himself.

I also wish to thank Laura Archer Coelho, for hiring me to be Philip K. Dick's literary executor; and Russell and Dorothy Balisok, Steven Harowitz, and Russell Galen, along with Laura, for being such a pleasure to work with and for their commitment to preserving PKD's literary legacy. My thanks to Andy Watson in particular, and all of the members of the Philip K. Dick Society, for being part of this work; and special thanks to Russell Galen, Jonathan Silverman, and the Scott Meredith Literary Agency, for their help in researching this book. Further thanks to the many people who've helped me research and write *Only Apparently Real,* in addition to those already mentioned: Donna Ansell, Kenta and Taiyo Williams, Clyde Taylor, Robert Lichtman, David and Joan May, Anne R. Dick, Kleo Mini, Nancy Hackett, Isa Hackett, David LaGraff, Joan Simpson, Lynne Cecil, Tim and Serena Powers, James Blaylock, Peter Pautz, Rick Bennett, Bob Stewart, Jay Kinney, John Wilton, Gregg Rickman, and especially to my editor, David G. Hartwell, who has a gift for being at the right place at the right time and making the right thing happen: he did it for Phil with *The Transmigration of Timothy Archer* and *The Divine Invasion* among many other books, and he's done it for me this time.

INTRODUCTION

To give a sense of who Philip K. Dick was or is, I must bring him into the present, or, if you prefer, bring you into his presence. Often what we feel when we are struck by a person's writing or music or art is the presence of that personality; Picasso is a good example. Some personalities dominate us completely by charming us constantly. This can be a problem in life or politics, but in the creative arts it is most desirable. Consider Mozart or Shakespeare. And such is the nature of charm that we often fail to notice that we have fallen under a spell.

A significant part of this book is a conversation with (and monologue by) a weaver of fictions, the novelist/philosopher (usually referred to as the science-fiction writer) Philip K. Dick, who died of a stroke in 1982 at the age of fifty-three, and left behind more than sixty books and an international cult following (and two cats and an apartment full of notes and five ex-wives and a steadily growing literary reputation).

The interview/conversation was recorded by the undersigned, Paul Williams, in 1974, in the course of writing a profile of PKD for *Rolling Stone* magazine. That profile appeared in the fall of 1975, and had the good fortune to be in the issue immediately following one of the most sensational scoops of the decade, *Rolling Stone*'s "Inside Story" of Patty Hearst's adventures on the road with the Symbionese Liberation Army. A lot of people bought *Rolling Stone* that week expecting the promised "Inside Patty" part two, and instead found themselves reading about this science-fiction writer whose home was broken into by the CIA, or was it Black Panthers, or Minutemen, or a godlike entity from another universe?

This book is conceived of as a sort of expansion of that profile, which apparently changed the lives of more than a few readers by getting them hooked on Dick. (Novelist William Gibson, who won the 1985 Philip K. Dick Memorial Award, writes of "the night we took the PKD and spent the next 48 hours looking for the way home to Base Reality.") Philip K. Dick has said his purpose as a novelist and a writer is to "pierce through the veil of what is only apparently real and get to what is really real." Again and again, in his work and in his life, he achieved this goal, only to find that it had to be done all over again, and things had perhaps gotten a little worse and a little less certain in the meantime.

Nothing is as it seems. This is a story about a man who experienced this and expressed it brilliantly and refused to stop there, devoting himself instead to the passionate and often comical search for what it is, if it isn't what it seems to be.

It's also a story about and conversation with a friend of mine. I knew Philip K. Dick for six years before I did these interviews, and seven years afterward. We laughed a lot together. When reality dissolves at your every glance, it furthers one to see the joke.

A CHRONOLOGICAL PREFACE

1928. *December 16.* Philip K. Dick and Jane C. Dick born at home, Chicago, Illinois.

1929. *January 26.* Jane Dick dies.

1929. *July.* Dick family to Johnstown, Colorado.

1929. *Autumn.* Dick family to California (Sausalito, then the Peninsula, then Alameda).

1931. Dick family to Berkeley, California.

1931. *Summer.* Phil in experimental nursery school.

1933. Phil's parents (Dorothy Grant Kindred Dick and Joseph Edgar Dick) divorced. Phil stays with mother.

1935. *January.* Phil and Dorothy to Washington, D.C.

1938. *June.* Phil and Dorothy return to California, settle in Berkeley.

1938. *Autumn.* Phil in Berkeley public school. Calls himself "Jim Dick."

1938. *December.* Publishes several editions of a dittoed newspaper, the *Daily Dick.* Address: 560 Colusa.

1940. *Summer.* Cazadero Music Camp. Now called "Phil" again. Classical-music enthusiast. Address: 1212 Walnut.

1941. Starts reading science fiction.

1942. *January 23.* First short story published, "Le Diable," in Young Authors' Club column, *Berkeley Daily Gazette.*

1942. Writes first novel, *Return to Lilliput.*

1942. *September.* Starts first and only year at California Preparatory School, Ojai.

1944. *Summer.* Starts working for Herb Hollis at University Radio, Shattuck Avenue, Berkeley.

1946–47. Phil's last year at Berkeley High School. Claustrophobia/agoraphobia. Weekly psychotherapy at Langley-Porter Clinic. Studies at home with tutor part of year. Address: 1711 Allston Way.

1947. *Autumn.* Enters, drops out of University of California, Berkeley.

1947. *December.* Moves out of mother's house for first

time, to apartment on Millvia with Jack Spicer, Robert Duncan, and others.

1948. Marries Jeanette Marlin. Divorced after six months. Address: Addison Street. (All addresses are Berkeley unless otherwise indicated.)

1949 (approx.). Called for the draft; rejected because of high blood pressure.

1949. Working at Art Music, Telegraph at Channing, Berkeley. Boss still Herb Hollis. Address: Bancroft Street, then (Dec. '49) 1931 Dwight Way.

1950. *May.* Buys house at 1126 Francisco Street, Berkeley.

1950. *June 14th.* Marries Kleo Apostolides.

1951. *November.* Phil sells first short story, "Roog," to Anthony Boucher for *The Magazine of Fantasy & Science Fiction.*

1952. *May.* Becomes client of the Scott Meredith Literary Agency.

1952. *May.* First story appears in print. ("Beyond Lies the Wub," *Planet Stories;* cover date July 1952.)

1952. Quits or is fired from Art Music.

Early 1950s. Phil and Kleo approached by FBI to attend Univ. of Mexico and collect information on student activities; they decline. Phil forms friendship with one agent, George Scruggs.

Early 1950s. Phil taking Serpasil for tachycardia, Semoxydrine (an amphetamine) for agoraphobia.

1953. *April 24th.* Dorothy Kindred marries Joseph Hudner after his wife, Dorothy's sister Marion, dies. Dorothy becomes stepmother of Marion and Joseph's children, Lynne and Neil Hudner.

1953. Thirty short stories published, including seven in one month. Writes *The Cosmic Puppets.*

1954. Twenty-eight stories published. Sells first novel, *Solar Lottery* (finished in March, sold in December). Attends science-fiction convention, August.

1955. Writes *Eye in the Sky.* First published novel, *Solar Lottery,* May.

1956–57. Writing mainstream only—no science fiction.

1957 (approx.). Offered job as scriptwriter for "Captain Video," good pay; refuses because unwilling/unable to go to New York City.

1958. Writing radio scripts for Mutual Broadcasting. Writes *Time Out of Joint,* first U.S. hardcover and first sale to U.S. publisher other than Ace.

1958. "Foster, You're Dead" published in *Ogonek,* large-circulation magazine, USSR.

1958. *September.* Phil and Kleo buy house in Point Reyes Station, Marin County; leave Berkeley.

1958. *October.* Phil meets Anne Rubenstein.

1958. *December.* Phil asks Kleo for divorce.

1959. *April 1.* Marries Anne Williams Rubenstein, in Mexico. Address: Box 176, Point Reyes Station.

1959. Writes *Confessions of a Crap Artist.*

1959. *December.* Contract with Harcourt Brace for mainstream novel.

1960. *February 25.* Laura Archer Dick born—Phil's first child, Anne's fourth.

1960. *December (approx.).* Phil gives up writing as a career, goes to work in Anne's jewelry business.

1961. *Autumn.* Writes *The Man in the High Castle.*

1963. *July.* Scott Meredith Agency returns Phil's mainstream novels as unsalable.

1963. *September.* Phil wins Hugo Award for Best Novel of the Year *(High Castle).*

1963–64. Writes ten science-fiction novels in less than two years.

1963. Phil and Anne start attending Episcopal church. Phil baptized.

1964. *March.* Phil files for divorce, moves to Berkeley.

1964. *June.* Living with Grania Davidson in Oakland. Address: 3919 Lyon Avenue, Oakland.

1964. *June.* Dislocates shoulder and totals his VW in auto accident.

1964. *Autumn.* Begins romance with Nancy Hackett.

1965. *October.* Divorce from Anne becomes final.

1966. *July 6.* Marries Nancy Hackett. Address: 57 Meadow Drive, San Rafael.

1966. Writes "Faith of Our Fathers," *Do Androids Dream of Electric Sheep?, Ubik.*

1966 or early '67. Visits Bishop Pike in Santa Barbara, participates in séance to contact Pike's dead son.

1967. *March 15.* Isolde ("Isa") Freya Dick born.

1967. *September.* Threatens to sue Terry Carr over a line in a fanzine.

1968. Sells option on film rights to *Androids.*

1968. Anthony Boucher dies.

1968. *June (approx.).* Nancy and Phil purchase house in Santa Venetia section of San Rafael. Address: 707 Hacienda Way.

1969. Bishop Pike dies.

1969. *August.* Hospitalized for pancreatitis.

1970. *July.* Writes *Flow My Tears.*

1970. *August.* Nancy leaves Phil, takes Isa.

1971. *November 17.* Break-in and burglary at Hacienda Way.

1972. *February.* Leaves San Rafael, flies to Vancouver, B. C., to be guest of honor at science-fiction convention; delivers speech, "The Android and the Human"; decides to stay in Canada.

1972. *March.* Suicide attempt; enters X-Kalay, heroin rehabilitation center, Vancouver.

1972. *April.* Leaves Canada, flies to Fullerton, southern California, to supervise archiving of manuscripts at California State University, Fullerton, and to start a new life.

1972. *July.* Meets Leslie ("Tessa") Busby. Address: 3028 Quartz Lane, Fullerton.

1973. *January.* Starts writing fiction again, after two-and-a-half-year hiatus, with short story, "A Little Something for Us Tempunauts."

1973. *April.* Marries Tessa (Leslie Busby).

1973. *July 25.* Christopher Kenneth Dick born.

1973. *Autumn.* New address: 1405 Cameo Lane, #4, Fullerton.

1974. *February/March.* Series of mystical experiences, as described in *Valis, Radio Free Albemuth,* the Exegesis, etc. Begins writing the Exegesis.

1974. *April.* Hospitalized for extremely high blood pressure.

1975. *May.* *Confessions of a Crap Artist* published.

1975. *Flow My Tears* wins the John W. Campbell Jr. Award for Best Novel of 1974.

1975. *Summer.* New address: 2461 Santa Ysabel, Fullerton.

1975. *October.* *Rolling Stone* profile appears.

1976. *February.* Tessa leaves with Christopher; Phil attempts suicide.

1976. Moves to Santa Ana to live with Doris Sauter. Address: 408 East Civic Center Drive, #C-1, Santa Ana.

1976. *September.* Doris moves out, takes apartment next door.

1977. *Summer.* Rents house in Sonoma, northern California, to live with Joan Simpson; doesn't give up Santa Ana apartment. Sonoma address: 550 Chase Street.

1977. *September.* Flies to Metz, France, with Joan Simpson, to be guest of honor at the Second International Festival of Science Fiction at Metz.

1977. *Autumn.* Resumes living full-time in Santa Ana.

1978. *August.* Dorothy Hudner (Phil's mother) dies.

1978. *October.* Writes introduction to *The Golden Man* ("The Lucky Dog Pet Store").

1978. *November.* Writes *Valis.*

1979. *September.* 408 Civic Center Drive becomes a condominium and Phil purchases his apartment.

1980. *April.* Writes "I Hope I Shall Arrive Soon" ("Frozen Journey"); sells to *Playboy* (first major-market short-story sale).

1981. *May.* Completes *The Transmigration of Timothy Archer.*

1981–82. Series of long interviews with Gregg Rickman, published posthumously.

1981. *June 29.* Sees first clip from *Blade Runner,* movie based on *Do Androids Dream,* on television.

1981. *September 23.* Writes "Tagore letter" for fanzine, *Niekas,* and mails copies to eighty-five correspondents.

1981. *PKD: A Philip K. Dick Bibliography,* by Daniel Levack, published.

1982. *February 18.* Suffers a paralyzing stroke and is hospitalized.

1982. *March 2.* Dies in Santa Ana.

CHAPTER ONE

> November 17, 1971. Philip K. Dick, a brilliant novelist well known in science-fiction circles, unlocked the front door of his house in San Rafael, California, and turned on the living-room lights. His stereo was gone. The floor was covered with water and pieces of asbestos. The fireproof, 1,100-pound asbestos-and-steel file cabinet that protected his precious manuscripts had been blown apart by powerful explosives.
>
> Thank God, he thought to himself. Thank God! I guess I'm not crazy after all.

Philip K. Dick and I collaborated on the above two paragraphs, the opening scene for my *Rolling Stone* profile, sometime during the three days I spent at his home in southern California, Halloween week, 1974. Dick's genius, during his short and remarkably prolific life, expressed itself best in science-fiction novels, but he also had a certain flair for self-dramatization. In his interviews and his many letters to correspondents all over the world (and his rare public appearances), he created himself as a character not so much out of as lost in the middle of one of his own novels.

Dick died of a stroke in March 1982. He was fifty-three

years old. He had been writing professionally for thirty years. During that time he produced at least forty-eight novels, of which thirty-four were published while he was alive. He also wrote more than a hundred short stories, a handful of essays and speeches, thousands of letters, and over a million words of obsessive commentary on the meaning of his mystical experiences in the spring of 1974.

Dick was largely unknown in the United States outside of science-fiction and academic circles until his death and the release of the movie *Blade Runner,* based on his novel *Do Androids Dream of Electric Sheep?* In Europe, Australia, and Japan, on the other hand, he has long been regarded as a major American novelist, a vitriolic visionary who sees through the surface of twentieth-century life and describes things as they really are. Had he lived, he might well have been nominated for a Nobel Prize.

My own fascination with Philip K. Dick's writing began at an interesting time in my life. I was nineteen, living in New York City, editing a popular/intellectual magazine about rock 'n' roll, and experimenting with LSD.

In the spring of 1967, I was on a flight from Boston to New York, returning from a Jefferson Airplane club appearance. I was reading Thomas Pynchon's *Crying of Lot 49,* which had just been released in paperback. My attention was taken by a very attractive blond woman sitting across the aisle and a few rows ahead of me. I was a shy, awkward teenager, and ordinarily I would have been terrified to approach her, but she was reading *God Bless You, Mr. Rosewater* by Kurt Vonnegut, Jr. I'd read everything by Vonnegut at least twice, and, scared as I was, I knew I couldn't pass up such a God-given opportunity.

So I met Trina Robbins, and back in New York she introduced me to Bhob Stewart and Art Spiegelman, and the three of them soon convinced me that Vonnegut, Pynchon, and the Rolling Stones notwithstanding, something truly vital was missing from my life if I wasn't reading Philip K.

Dick. I think it was Bhob who sealed my fate, in some Lower East Side apartment, by reading me two pages from *Time out of Joint.*

The funny thing was that I already knew Bhob Stewart, although I hadn't seen him for four years. And I knew Trina by reputation as soon as she told me her name on the airplane. These people and I used to belong to a secret society together, back in the dim past (it's odd to have a dim past when you're only nineteen), called science-fiction fandom. That meeting in midair reawakened my connection with the extended underworld of science-fiction readers and fans, and so it wasn't so odd that slightly more than a year later, in August 1968, I found myself on the floor of a smoke-filled room in Oakland, California, at the twenty-sixth World Science Fiction Convention, introducing myself to Philip K. Dick.

Print-oriented person that I am, I had a prop, like Vonnegut on the airplane, to help me overcome my shyness at invading the privacy of this writer who had become an awesome figure to me over the past fifteen months. What I had was an article I had written about Dick for an obscure underground newspaper called *New York Avatar.* Phil read it while we sat there, and we ate animal tranquilizers together and became fast friends.

I'm going to share some sections from that article with you now (it was originally published as part of a column called "Thrilling Wonder Stories") because it records my first impressions of Philip K. Dick and suggests to me that I knew him almost as well before I met him as I do now after fourteen years of friendship and three years of serving as his literary executor. Here's what I wrote in the spring of 1968:

> Philip K. Dick is this paranoid guy who writes fascinating paranoid novels full of objects that talk and realities that vanish. I've never met the man, but I remember some garbled story about him stealing a friend's diapers off his

porch in Berkeley, or maybe Dick was accusing the friend of stealing *his* diapers; I admit I wasn't paying much attention at the time. But now I read (in *The Game-Players of Titan*) that paranoia is "the involuntary reception of other people's suppressed hostile and aggressive thoughts," and I wonder if here we have a man who is thoroughly rational only at his typewriter, where he has time to make his actions fit together before displaying them to the world. Such a person should not be frowned upon; an "ordinary" person, one who spends his time and energy making the everyday world feel certain of his sanity, seldom has time to do anything else. Those who let themselves be thought crazy are at least trying to focus their energies in more constructive directions.

. . . Phil Dick is not only aware of the ambivalence of sanity but has very real doubts about the existence of the world around him. In *Time out of Joint* a soft-drink stand with all the trimmings eloquently disintegrates before the protagonist in a moment of stopped time, leaving only a scrap of paper with the words SOFT DRINK STAND printed on it. In *The Three Stigmata of Palmer Eldritch* you wake from a psychedelic trip into another psychedelic trip, in which everyone and everything in the world, including yourself, slowly and inexorably turns out to be the person who first took the drug. And in *The Game-Players of Titan,* "The vug said, 'Mr. Garden, when did you first begin to notice these disembodied feelings, as if the world about you is not quite real?' " The poor protagonist is going through a perfectly ordinary, albeit exceedingly clever, space-opera adventure, and would be quite all right except that the author, and all the other characters in the novel, continually try to psychoanalyze him.

. . . So we have a form of fiction in which author—as personified in the protagonist—pits himself against author—the clever guy who keeps changing the nature of the world around the protagonist. And don't think Dick, who writes much of his stuff on amphetamine, doesn't enjoy every aspect of the conflict. Jim Morrison sings, "I used to play a game . . . called go insane"; which is true—what you do, what Jim did, is just say "Whoops, I'm out of control," and let yourself do whatever strange thing you feel like doing, let all those C*razY energies come to the surface and carry you away.

And, yes, you're completely out of control, irrational, but choosing to lose control was a thoroughly rational act. Jim Morrison isn't crazy—he just doesn't care sometimes; and I would accuse both Phil Dick and myself of similar transgressions, channeled in somewhat different directions.

. . . Dick's world is a world of specific ambiguity, not the shimmering general ambiguity of songwriter Van Dyke Parks, where you know that everything is or could be all things, but a sinister paranoid world where each thing seems to be one way and then turns out to maybe be another, and eventually it becomes clear that you can't be certain of anything—since each of us perceives a different world, really large-scale communication breakdown and even sanity breakdown are possible and, in a Dick novel, probable. But only because he starts from the premise that we *are* communicating, that things are a certain way, and then goes on to demonstrate/discover that they're not. If you start (as Parks does in *Song Cycle*) from the idea that nothing is known and that there is nothing that *needs* to be known, then you can go on and ambiguously create a world of multileveled meanings and realities in which whatever meanings you happen to pick out are there as a gift, are good to know about—starting from uncertainty, everything is just kind of a nice more-than-nothing and ambiguity is simply a way of life, a pleasant adaptation to indefinite surroundings. Reading a P. K. Dick novel from the back probably wouldn't be scary at all, but I guess Phil's never done that. He's written a lot of books, and I admit to only having read a small handful, but each one that I have read starts from sanity. And of course falls apart. But somehow he never learns, you see what I mean?—having discovered incoherence and general difficulty in perceiving the universe everywhere he looks, he still never comes back and starts a new story from the vantage point of chaos is reigning and what the hell. He insists on returning to an apparently stable Go, maybe because if you lose it all on Boardwalk every time around, you just can't pass up that free $200.

I don't know what Phil was thinking as he lay on that hotel-room floor (we, along with other friends at the convention, had taken what we were told was synthesized THC, the active ingredient in marijuana; it turned out to be a horse tranquilizer called PCP, which showed up a decade later to plague American cities and suburbs under the name "angel dust") and read my nineteen-year-old ravings. Probably he was flattered to be written about somewhere other than in a science-fiction magazine. Certainly he felt some satisfaction and excitement at being embraced by the "counterculture."

I saw him a number of times over the next few years, always at his house in San Rafael. (Phil was a recluse and probably attended less than a dozen science-fiction conventions and book-signing parties during his entire career.) Two incidents stand out in my mind.

One was when he gave me the manuscript of his unpublished mainstream novel *Confessions of a Crap Artist,* his favorite among the many non-science-fiction novels he wrote and couldn't sell in the 1950s. I had offered to try to find a publisher for it among my contacts in New York. Phil paced the floor, and finally asked the *I Ching* for its advice on this venture. The oracle answered, "Bites on old dried meat and strikes on something poisonous." This seemed ominous to me. Phil kept berating his young wife, Nancy, for being too cheerful; he seemed contemptuous of her involvement with some kind of positive-thinking philosophy. He was nervous, hostile, unhappy. Then, mysteriously, his mood shifted. In retrospect I think it was very stressful for him to try again with this old, beloved novel that had been rejected so many times. It brought up a lot of hopes and fears, and memories of disappointment.

The other incident was actually a phone call. For a brief period in the spring of 1969, about ten days, I traveled with Timothy and Rosemary Leary, ostensibly as campaign adviser for Tim's effort to become governor of California. We ended up, after a college lecture in California, a rock festival in Florida, and a press conference in New York City, in Montreal, where John Lennon and Yoko Ono were performing their "Bed-In for Peace." While in New York I bought a hardcover copy of PKD's novel *Ubik,* just published, and it turned out Leary was also a great fan of Phil's novels. I arranged for Tim Leary to call Phil Dick from John Lennon's hotel room. Later we gave Lennon a copy of Phil's *The Three Stigmata of Palmer Eldritch.* Apparently he read it, because he told an interviewer he wanted to make a movie of it.

Years went by. I moved to a hippie commune in the Canadian wilderness, then back to New York City. Phil's wife left him, and he got very involved with the "street people" in San Rafael—kids, many of them doing drugs, who would use his house as a place to hang out or crash. I visited him once during this period and got the impression he was playing a kind of guru role. It was a weird scene.

In November 1972 I received a letter from Phil:

> Oh Paul, it's so good to hear from you, my friend. Awful things happened to me since I saw you. Somebody just about got me back about a year ago; I came home and found my files blown open with plastic military explosives, windows smashed in, doorlocks smashed, everything of value gone such as stereo, business records and cancelled checks, correspondence and papers gone, rubble everywhere. . . . I never was able to really live there afterward because of the loss and damage. I got threatening phone calls later saying the next time it'd be worse. Two County Sheriff's Dept inspectors came out, a lot of photos were taken, investigation and like that—one arrest much later, of a Panther, with my gun stolen from my files that night: I had bought it to protect myself, knowing the hit was coming.
>
> I still don't know who or why exactly; I've heard many theories. In the wet rubble on the floors: big combat boot footprints. A bunch of guys made the hit. They worked fast and noisy. One informed theory: nearby Birchers, the Minutemen. It was a military-like operation, what they call search

and seize I believe. The police informally said, "We don't want a crusader here in Marin County. You better move away or you'll get a bullet in your back some night. Or worse." I asked what the "or worse" was and the police sergeant said, "You wouldn't want to know." I did what he suggested. I moved out of the county, all the way to Canada. I've never been back.

There were a couple of hostile people operating around me at the time, but I thought they were undercover narcotics agents and handled them as such. Evidently I was wrong. This is a story I've never told, a story I'm afraid, even a year later, to tell. Someday I'll tell it, but my fear is enormous. I was told I wouldn't live to give my speech at Vancouver. "If you don't," I was told, "someone posing as you will deliver it for you." Just remembering back I start shaking. I really didn't expect to live to February, and told people so, but not why.

I was shucked by deadly people playing a deadly game: I saw a lot of guns, explosives, silencers—they used blackmail on me, terror and psychological intimidation. It damn near worked. They threatened me with arrest and tried to set me up again and again on entrapment. Shit, Paul; I can't write about it any more, even to you. It was so fucking awful. They even tried to involve me in murder, conspiracy to commit murder, saying it was the only way I could save my own life. But I did get away. The fear remains, especially now because by chance I've gotten hold of more information about this illegal secret paramilitary organization that was hounding me there in Marin County, and I think I know what it consisted of. Not Minutemen or Panthers either one. Paul, it is a neo-Nazi group.

CHAPTER TWO

Philip K. Dick has said that he started writing his first novel when he was thirteen. It was called *Return to Lilliput,* and although no manuscript survives, it was almost certainly a further adventure of Gulliver, in the tradition of Jonathan Swift.

This scrap of information about Dick's first effort casts light on his entire career: He was attracted to fantasy, fantastic stories, and chose to express himself in that realm; he saw himself firmly in a literary tradition, although one that was often obscure to his contemporaries; he was precocious, ahead of his time; he saw himself as a satirist, saw fiction as an opportunity to take an overview of contemporary society and, on a broader level, of humankind (the sort of overview that becomes most effective when focused in on individual humans who happen to have universal, Everyman, characteristics). He was ambitious. He was a humorist, like Swift. And he wrote about a sort of small land filled with little people, people he cared about, and he as author was peering in, watching and listening with fascination, writing it all down. Later, at age twenty-eight, he wrote a mainstream (i.e., not overtly fantastic) novel about the misfortunes of a TV repairman and called it *Puttering About in a Small Land.*

Also at the age of thirteen Philip Dick became a published writer, beginning a long series of appearances in the Young Authors' Club column of the *Berkeley Daily Gazette* with a short story called "Le Diable."

For the next forty years Dick wrote almost constantly, and most of what he submitted for publication—with the frustrating exception of his mainstream novels—was published. In the years since his untimely death in 1982, his career has blossomed further with the publication of many previously ignored manuscripts, making him appear even more prolific in death than in life. In 1985 five new books by Philip K. Dick were published in hardcover in the United States.

In the case of Philip K. Dick we have—like Proust, but with a twist, a difference—a life lived on paper. He was a hermit; he suffered from anxieties and phobias, which became acute at those times in his life when he felt forced to participate with others (i.e., going to school and holding a job). He had many friends, was very charming and caring in person and on the phone, and his life was focused almost obsessively around other people, mostly women; yet his life focused even more obsessively on the projections of his mind and heart that he could place on paper: letters (and he kept carbons of almost every letter he ever wrote), novels, short stories, *I Ching* readings, essays, and endless discussions with himself, often handwritten, sometimes seemingly as much as fifty or perhaps a hundred pages of small, handwritten print in one night.

It isn't that he recorded his entire life on paper—relatively little of his work is directly autobiographical—but rather that so much of his life energy went into the act of writing. He lived to communicate, and perhaps he communicated with such energy and passion because he was never quite sure he'd been heard or, indeed, that he'd said what he wanted to say. He enjoyed quite a bit of success and even adulation during his lifetime; and yet right up to the last year of his life, he would answer fan letters—not every time, but several times a year—with an impassioned note saying, in effect, "You are the first person who has ever really understood what I'm doing!" or "Your letter got me through an incredible block and has changed the course of my life and my career!" And he was sincere; all the evidence is that he totally believed this letter every time he wrote it. When your belief is that no one is hearing you, it comes as a revelation each time your defenses are penetrated and someone actually momentarily reaches you with the message that you reached them.

But doubt always returns. For Dick it was a creative force. The plots of most of his science-fiction novels are moved from page to page by doubt and by the collapse of the characters' and author's assumptions as to what is going on, forcing new hypotheses and new plot developments. And what makes these books so rich is that Dick continually is able to come up with new twists, new theories, new possibilities to explore—his inability to experience the solidity of any one reality becomes fertile soil for the creation of endless alternate realities, each at least as convincing as the one that went before.

The same process can be seen in the theological/philosophical study that occupied the last eight years of his life. He had a series of intensely powerful mystical experiences in February and March of 1974, and spent much of his time thereafter writing down, in letters or on notepaper, his theories and analyses of what had actually happened, and what it meant.

Each evening he would get a great new hypothesis and explore it with gusto, certain that he had gotten to the bottom of this, determined to write down all his thoughts about it while it was still fresh in his mind—and then the next evening a new thought would come along, maybe preceded by doubts about his previous conclusions, or even by an overwhelming sense that everything he'd assumed and written down so far was garbage. And so he would find himself pursuing the new thought, new line of analysis, new possibility. He lived for the pursuit of truth, and the world in which that pursuit took place was for him the world of pen or typewriter (or sometimes tape recorder, usually when he was being interviewed) and paper.

And notice that it is not that he pursued the thought and then wrote down his conclusions. He pursued *by* writing—that is the realm where the action took place, that is where he lived so much of his life.

Because he experienced his thoughts and feelings via the act of writing, and then preserved what he'd written, the man's aliveness, his feelings and his thought processes, remain with us now, years after his death, in the form of letters, novels, notes—not a record of his experiences, if you catch the distinction I'm making, but the experience itself.

This is also true, of course, of the interview transcribed in this book. Phil is speaking to me, trying to impress me, give me what I want, make me laugh, convince me of something, etc., etc., and at the same time he is very aware of the tape recorder running and the likelihood that some of what he's saying will be printed in *Rolling Stone.* He is definitely speaking to me, and at the same time he's performing for a larger audience. He knows you're out there. If you get the feeling at times, reading these conversations, that he's speaking directly to you, you're probably right. He may not have known you'd be reading him in a book instead of a magazine, but he knew he wanted to reach you.

These conversations, in other words, are an opportunity for the reader to go on a strange sort of adventure, to get inside a person's mind, to experience a different way of thinking, and to be part of this drama, Phil's effort to identify and express the truth. It is the differentness of his way of thinking that is so fascinating; yet, paradoxically, there is for many of us a familiarity about this differentness, a feeling that it's my differentness, too, and he's expressing it for me. This more than anything, I think, is what makes his readers so passionately loyal to him. Reading Philip K. Dick makes us feel less alone in the world.

It would have given Phil a lot of pleasure to know that his writing helped to ease even one person's loneliness. Perhaps the most formative event in his life was the death of his twin sister, six weeks after they were born. He spent the next fifty-three years looking for her, reaching out to her, missing her, creating her.

CHAPTER THREE

THE BREAK-IN

CONVERSATION, *October 30, 1974*

PAUL WILLIAMS: As a folk hero, you have to tell me again about how your house was broken into.

PHILIP K. DICK: That'll make me a folk hero?

W: Sure. That's what we're doing this year.

D: Um. Jeez, man. Um. Um. I've always hoped somebody would ask me that. You know, I've been waiting for somebody to come here, turn on a tape recorder, and ask me that. I've rehearsed it. I've—

W: Do you do it different ways at different times?

D: Well, I've—I've shaped it into an absolutely authentic record of what happened. I wrote the ACLU and they're looking into it.

W: What are they looking into?

D: They're looking into how come . . . You know, I'm not as garrulous as I thought. I mean, I'm garrulous, verbose even—

W: You've already filled two tapes, plus one that we erased. . . . [laughter]

D: But I mean, when it comes to certain topics, a certain reticence hits. I don't want to babble mindlessly at this point.

W: [laughs]

D: Ah, ah, I mean to continue to babble mindlessly.

W: As opposed to other points at other places . . .

D: Yeah, right. Um. What was the question? You can see how I got away from the police when I was interrogated, can't you?

W: Let's see. What was the question?

D: Yeah. Could I come back to—

W: On November 17, 1971—

D: Oh, Jesus. Where was I? Do you know, they read me that as an accusation, that I was calling the cops too much? When they told me I had to get out of Marin County or be shot. They said, "You know you call the cops all the time? Like look on November 17, 1971. There you were calling us up." I said, "Well, for God's sake, I came home, my house was in ruins, my files were blown up, my papers were gone, my stereo was gone, the windows were smashed in, the doorknobs were smashed off, the hasps were pulled off—with rubble all over the floor." I said, "Of course I called you."

He said, "Now let's go on to the next one. You called us three days later." I said, "Yeah, no cops would come out and look at it." And they said there had been no robbery in that area. No report of a robbery.

W: But you reported a robbery.

D: Oh, sure, I reported it.

W: What happened? Where were you? Were you out eating at the local McDonald's?

D: Well, okay. I could tell it chronologically, I guess. Um . . . I was living with this girl. Her name was Barbara. And one evening . . . We had a lot of picture windows, which looked out onto the gardens and everything.

W: This was on Hacienda Way?

D: Yes. And suddenly she said, "Phil, this house is gonna be hit. People are gonna break in, I can tell, I can feel 'em out there." And I said, "You're crazy, Barbara." And I continued to tell her that. Each day, each night she'd say, "I can feel 'em, I can feel 'em getting into position. I know they're out there."

I said, "Okay, here's what I'll do." I called the police. And had them scan the yard, you know, search out the yard with flashlights. They found nothing. I called the utility company to come on a pretext, so they'd be in the yard, clomping around.

One time I looked up, I saw a shape run through the next yard in the darkness. That told me she was right. It was three A.M., this guy's running as fast as he could go. That was enough. So I got her out of there. I moved her to a friend's house. And I also—I bought a gun. Matter of fact, the cops had suggested that I buy a gun.

W: At what point did they suggest that you buy a gun?

D: That was sometime earlier, when I had called them, I forget what for. They said, "You know, you ought to buy yourself a gun. We're not going to do anything to help you. We haven't got the time to come out. If you were to call about something, our man might be somewhere else." I says, "Your *man!*" I says, "What am I calling, a plumbing firm?" They say, "Well, I'll tell you, protecting yourself is up to you." So I was already looking into buying a gun anyway, on their recommendation. They said, "You're going to need one."

W: What did they know about you at this point?

D: That I was a troublemaker.

W: That a lot of people came and went from your house, a lot of young people?

D: Yeah. . . . There'd been a lot of trouble at my place, a lot of freaks there, and a lot of calls for assistance from me.

The purchase of a new gun requires a five-day waiting period in California. But because I felt this girl was right, I bought a used gun, to have it immediately. I got her out, got a guy in with me who was pretty tough, and—he was there I think forty-eight hours and, ah, we had some kind of hassle and he took off. So I was alone again.

It was time to go shop for dinner, I had to shop by car—there's no store close enough to go on foot. I locked my gun in my files—the guy that sold me the gun said I should lock it up when I left, which is really good advice.

W: File cabinets?

D: Yeah, these were eleven-hundred-pound fireproof file cabinets—it wasn't a safe, but it was a Mosler class D filing system with locks and heavy asbestos and steel sheets to hold off fire; it was fireproof rather than burglarproof.

I put the gun in and locked it up and got in the car and as soon as I'd driven a couple of blocks I could tell something was seriously wrong with the car, I mean black smoke was pouring out of it and it would barely go. And I know enough about cars to know that the car had been sabotaged, and that I had a choice of turning back, abandoning the car and going back on foot, or trying to get out of there. I elected to get out of there. I just floorboarded it and drove it as far as I could and abandoned it. And I was near enough to a doctor's house that I knew to go there.

I spent hours trying to get a tow truck to come and get my car—they wouldn't come and get it, for some reason. And then I spent hours trying to get somebody to drive me home, and I couldn't do it, and then I couldn't get a cab! So I walked most of the way home, and then I went to a bar and called a cab from there. So there was about four hours, from six to ten o'clock at night, that I was gone.

I got home about ten, by cab, and unlocked the front door, and the house was a shambles. The floor was covered with wet asbestos from the files, just covered with it.

W: Wet?

D: Wet, yeah.

W: Where'd that come from?

D: Well, took me a while to figure that out. All I could see was rubble. My stereo was gone, windows smashed in, and just, you know, like World War Two.

W: The window was broken in?

D: Yeah, and also screens torn—it was a number of entry tries that had failed. I had nailed shut many of the windows, nailed them partially shut, and put locks on the doors, safety locks, and they had failed entry points there. So they had smashed in one window—and in coming in and finding doors shut, they had smashed the knobs and locks right off the doors. The noise must have been quite severe at that point, doing that, must have been quite loud.

And the file had been blown— Well, I turned and got the cab, ran back and got the cabdriver to come and look at it, and—we'd talked on the way, he was a real tough dude, he was a biker—he took one look at it and said, "I won't go in that house."

I says, "I want you to talk to the police." He says, "I won't come in, I'll wait in the cab, that's the best I'll do." And I got his number, but he drove off. He was scared shitless.

I called the cops on the phone. It was a long time before they came out. First they wouldn't come at all. They said, "We're too busy." Then finally a whole bunch of 'em came out. By that time I'd had a chance to look around. The water was from towels that had been soaked in water; they were all heaped up in the bathroom shower and it was easy to see that they had been put over the file when it was blown.

And that's why the asbestos was wet, 'cause the asbestos was from the file. And a lot of the contents of the files that hadn't been taken were wet. Photographs were all water-soaked.

W: They put it over, what's that do? Safety, for themselves?

D: Well, I found out later from a guy that had been in Special Forces that what they used was a military explosive called C3 or C4. It's quite different from the commercial explosives used by safecrackers. What it does is, they—I saw in the files two holes drilled with big bits, great big bits, I found broken bits all around. And this plas—it's a plastic explosive, and it's pushed down, and then they soak towels, as I found, and put them over it. And when it explodes, it throws a sheet of flame through the room but makes no noise.

But this sheet of flame has to be damped, by water, and it turns the water and the towels to steam. But that's it, it's all over, and the windows are not blown, which is why the windows around my file were not blown. But that's a military explosive, and this was 1971, and at that point none of this plastic explosive was in the hands of the underground, this guy said. I asked him, when did this get in the hands of the underground? He said, oh, '72 on. C3 or C4. The same that was used recently in the L.A. airport by terrorists.

And this Special Forces guy said to me, he said, "You couldn't have known"—from my description, he said it was C3 or C4—he said, "You couldn't have known that unless you were in Special Forces." He said, "I was a demolitions expert. I used that. I was decorated for using that." He said, "You couldn't have known that you'd find water-soaked towels."

W: Was this in a separate room that you had these files?

D: This was in my study, yeah. And the files had been gone through thoroughly.

W: What was missing?

D: It was almost impossible to establish because all my papers were in it, except for what was in the desk. . . . When I went in the bedroom I found that my dresser drawers and the closets had been gone through, too, for papers. They had dumped what they didn't take on the bed.

They had taken every canceled check in the house, going back over twenty years. They had gotten every single one. That had taken quite a bit of time. And they knew just where to look. And, uh, I have no theory about why they did that.

But that was one of the objects of this search. And some books were missing, as a matter of fact.

W: No manuscripts?

D: No completed manuscripts, no, but there were a lot of short, single papers, holographic notes that were missing.

When the police came they told me to make up the burglary list while I was not in the house; I mean, the house was not inhabitable. And I said I would go stay with friends. And they said, "Okay, well, have the burglary list, the list of what was stolen, by tomorrow morning; come into the police station." I said, "How can I tell unless I stay here?" They said, "Well, that's your problem." I had to draw the list up while I was away.

I have the list, I still have a copy of the list, and it shows that it was business papers, plus stereo. Jewelry was left, jewelry was not taken.

W: They took the entire stereo system?

D: Yes. Which was pretty valuable. I had Fender Bassman bottoms, four fifty-inch speakers, and a Sansui amplifier. In the file were things like amethysts—amethyst jewelry. They didn't take 'em, they were lying right there. It was obvious right away that it was papers that they were interested in.

And, um—they had wiped the floor, so that there were no footprints. Because of the wet asbestos all over, there would have been footprints everywhere. I found a footprint in a closet, though, that they had missed, and it showed combat boots.

W: What about the rest of the house?

D: They didn't touch the contents of either desk. Or at least they didn't take anything. They were very selective, they seemed to know their way around the house. The police pointed that out. Some closets were never touched at all.

W: The police did come at some point?

D: Yes, after about half an hour, a number of police came.

But they merely strolled through and just observed. Tools were taken, valuable tools were taken. I could see no pattern in it.

W: Some obvious valuables were skipped?

D: Right.

W: You didn't have any money in the house?

D: No. I could never establish a pattern except that the canceled checks was the only thing for sure, since it required them to go through drawers, boxes—you know how many canceled checks you acquire in twenty-one years. . . . And they'd taken a sample checkbook of every checking account they could find, of new checks, unused checks.

W: Let me ask this: They passed over some valuables, calling into question whether or not they were—and obviously the checks don't fit in with a simple robbery thing. Now, looking at it from another point of view, suppose it was just somebody who was angry at you, having a feud with you, in some way . . .

D: This is what I assumed it was. This is what my friends assumed it was. There were so many feuds going on in my circle that my friends who looked at it thought it was other friends of mine who had done it. And this was of course a possibility, of a grudge thing—you know, it had a grudge quality.

W: And it wouldn't necessarily follow a logical pattern.

D: Right. Just that it was disruptive, just that it was a disruptive thing.

Um . . . One of the things—the first thing that made me think that there might be something more to it—was that when I took the list of what was stolen into the police department the next morning, they refused the list, telling me there'd been no burglary the night before. The logbook showed nothing.

W: Different cops than the night before?

D: Yeah, this would be the desk, yeah. But nonetheless

they had stressed the night before, you see, the importance of this list; and enough cops had come out—there wouldn't have been any problem establishing that there'd been a robbery. I told the girl at the desk that they were wrong, and that they should send somebody out to investigate. Several days went by and nobody came out. So I called in, and they told me again that there had been no robbery there.

And I told them then that they would have to send somebody out, that it was not a robbery, that it was more severe than a robbery, that it was more in the nature of a kind of hit-search-and-seize operation. 'Cause by that time my lawyer had come out and looked at it and so described it; he described it as the kind of thing that military training—that he had had in the service, they were taught to do it.

W: Were there any Vietnam vets among the people that were coming and going at your house?

D: None. Not one. So at that point two police inspectors immediately came out, together. Instantly came out. And they—one of them accused me of having done it myself.

W: These are again people you didn't—different policemen still.

D: Right.

W: This was just his offhand—as he presented it, anyway, just an idea that he had when he went out there?

D: Uh, after looking about he smiled and asked me why I'd done it.

And then I got really sore. He looked around and he says, "Well, what I really," he says, "what I wonder is why did you scatter the asbestos all around, why did you do *that?*" And laughed. And I just saw red. And I just told him—now it's hard to talk to an inspector anyway. And I said, "I wasn't insured, I had no insurance." I said, "Why the hell would I do a thing like this?" I said, "You guys are really crazy. You got no record of a robbery, you tell me that I did it, my house is a shambles, I can't live in it. Look at this file's been blown up." And so on.

So they then had police photographers come out and take photographs. And one of the two inspectors who was assigned told me that he was in charge of the case. And to show him any drill bits I could find, things like that, and so forth.

Now see, the case was officially cracked by that inspector. He used that expression, he cracked the case.

W: He decided there really was a burglary and that somebody really did do it.

D: Yeah. And it came from the house behind. He showed me how he knew. All the important points of entry were in the rear. And there was boards missing from the fence. And I had noticed that the house behind was empty that night, which was unusual. They had ten children. They were never all gone. That house was empty that night and remained empty for one week. So I could have told him that. I knew that. And that's where I saw the guy running, was in that yard.

W: And who lived in that house?

D: Uh—and this is off the record. [After so many years, and with PKD's death, I've decided this no longer needs to be off the record. What's interesting is that Phil chose to make it "off the record" in the first place. And it reminds us that he remained conscious that he was not just talking to a friend; he was talking to a reporter from *Rolling Stone*.] A black family, which I was very friendly with. But it turned out later, I was told, the police showed me pictures of some of those guys, they were in San Quentin and they were terrorists. [Phil had this way of speaking very dramatically, his voice would get lower, he'd bend forward a little and get real serious.]

W: According to the police.

D: Yes. Look at the position it put me in. And the guy caught with the gun—they caught a guy with the gun, they said—was a black guy. And from separate sources, reliable sources, he was a Panther. You see? They had—the police information was it came from the house behind. That doesn't make it the black guys, though. It just means where it came from. That doesn't prove anything but the location. They could've arrested and moved them out, for all I know. But on separate information, the guy that was arrested with the gun—he was arrested by another police agency. I checked into it.

W: Did they ask you to file charges, or anything like that?

D: On the contrary. That's when the curtain of silence fell.

W: They didn't ask you to identify the gun?

D: They just asked me to tell them the serial number and the length of the barrel.

W: And they said okay, it's the same gun, and then?

D: Well, then later I asked—I wrote and asked if the man had come to trial, and if he'd come to trial, what the results were. If any of the other stuff had been recovered. And I was never able to get any more information from—never even got an answer.

W: Did the people move back into that house?

D: Yes. After a week or so they moved back.

W: The same family.

D: Yes. And I saw the guy who had been arrested with the gun drive up and park there and talk to them, and he did know them. He was in the area, and the black lady across the street identified his car to me as the car she'd seen parked in front of the house that night.

W: So you did talk to that family?

D: No, I didn't. I talked to the black people across the street from me. That is, another family. And I saw his car pull up. So there's no doubt about it, it was the car parked there that night, and it was him, and he did know the people in the house behind me. It all fitted independent of police information. And it did synchronize with police information.

W: Was this neighborhood, uh, more black than white?

D: It was becoming black. And a lot of the blacks were militant. Very militant. I found out that they'd driven out the white people who owned the house ahead of me, previous to me, at knifepoint; and they were generally driving the whites out to a certain extent. But they'd always treated me very well, and I'd had a very good friendship with these guys.

W: What about the possibility that this was part of, you know, of driving you out? I mean the break at the house.

D: That's correct. That's very possible. That is very possible. But it's not proved [voice rising], it's not a QED thing, by any means. The police showed me pictures of the black guys in the house behind, they asked me to identify them. I couldn't do it, as a matter of fact—didn't have that much contact with those particular guys. Matter of fact, they were in Q at the time, San Quentin, so they told me, and I recognized the names. They were the correct people behind me, but they were gone by then.

Um . . . When this SLA thing came up, recently, reading the background on that, I realized that it's quite possible this was black terrorists that drove me out 'cause I was white. It's quite possible. It's even possible that I knew some of them, 'cause some of the blacks there who were militant blacks had been friends—in fact I'd hired two of them, in the previous weeks, to protect a girl that was, uh, a junkie pusher was trying to kill. I hired two of them to protect her, to drive around behind her and see that he didn't get her.

W: Did they have any familiarity with the inside of the house?

D: No. Not at all like what would have been required for that burglary, like the checks, the location of them.

W: None of those people did?

D: No, none of those black guys did anything. They came into the living room for a moment, they came in the study for a moment, one of them saw me open the file. The black guys also knew I was completely broke. I had to borrow all the money that I paid them for protecting that girl. They knew I was destitute, I didn't have a cent. And they certainly didn't know where the checks were, you know, in the other room.

W: Were any of these people involved with Nancy [Phil's wife; they had been separated for more than a year at the time of the break-in] in some way?

D: Yes. They were close friends.

W: Which, the people who lived—

D: In the house behind, yes. And the people across the street.

W: At this point you were broken up with Nancy already?

D: Correct. She'd gone off with the guy across the street, the black guy across the street. It turned out, I was told later, that he was a militant black and was into a lot of violent stuff. And he was close friends with the—

W: He was never accused in connection with this thing?

D: No. But they were all friends. I know that from firsthand knowledge. And I was tipped off repeatedly, by disinterested people who had nothing to gain, that the guy that Nancy went off with was involved with militant, possibly terrorist, black groups, possibly ones that hit my house.

So that is certainly a very high degree of possibility. It's possible, but it doesn't account for the most mysterious thing of all. If this were the case—now this was at the time of the Angela Davis trial; these people were hated by the police there, these black militants. I cannot see, then, why, if these people did it, that the police would show no enthusiasm for pursuing the cause of this robbery, this burglary. Would not really look into it, would openly accuse me of having done it and falsified the whole situation, and would refuse even to answer repeated written questions as to whether there had been a trial and recovery of anything.

That is, I can't understand what they would gain, then. Because they were so determined to break the militant black Left, there, in that area. You'd think that this would be exactly what they would want.

There is one possibility, though, which was suggested to

me by a very astute person recently in appraising all this. A possibility that never occurred to me. It's a theoretical thing, it's an idea to explain these two things, the fact that there's a great deal of evidence to point to the fact that this was done by militant blacks who wanted to make that a black area, who resented me there, who resented my association with blacks. That was another thing: One black chick said, "There's blacks here that don't like you talking to blacks"—to explain that, and the police hostility towards me, and the fact that finally the police said, "If you don't move out of here, you're gonna get shot."

W: The police felt that you were a "nigger lover"?

D: Yes . . . that's—that's right—

W: Something along those lines.

D: Yeah, right, because I, you know, that's one possibility—that they figured I got what I deserved.

W: They didn't want to get involved.

D: That considering the kind of person I was, that's what I deserved to have happen to me.

But this guy suggested an even more startling thought, which I really kind of think might be true. He said, as regards the robbery, it is quite possible that the robbery was done by the authorities, hoping to find evidence that I had direct links with black militants, so that I could be shown to be part of black terrorist militant political Left groups. By letters from known radicals, letters from people like the Berrigans, so that I could be tried for being part of the Angela Davis Communist hippie black thing.

So that the robbery was by the authorities, looking for that kind of evidence, you see? That behind my published writings lay correspondence that would be incriminating. And canceled checks, he claims—that would be a major thing they would look for. Checks written out to people. Also, you know, funds that I had—

W: There were a lot of people coming and going from the

house, a lot of things happening there . . . it's possible the police suspected there was some kind of organization here—

D: That's possible, and that may be what they were looking for evidence of.

W: Could be anything that they couldn't figure out what it was . . . It obviously wasn't something ordinary, in their way of seeing it.

D: Absolutely. I was an intellectual writer, and why . . . Whereas actually . . .

W: These street people.

D: Yeah, street people. Heads. Hippies. And what these kids did was sat around and played cards and listened to the Grateful Dead at top volume for hours, and did nothing at all that I could see, if you see what I mean. Certainly weren't interested in politics.

Yeah, right. This all fits in. You can see their view. You can see how it would—and the authorities would never be sure until they actually got into the house and got a look at the correspondence. Once they blew the files, got a look at all the canceled checks, and the correspondence, and so forth. The house was not just robbed. The house was searched. And then while I was in Canada, all my remaining business papers disappeared. All of them. From both desks. The contents of both desks.

W: Really?

D: Every single thing. And the desks. Disappeared.

W: Is there some reason that your wife would have wanted that stuff?

D: Well, there's only one possibility, and that was something that the bank and I were considering, the possibility that there were forgeries going through my account.

W: But were there? That's something that you would be able to find out if there were.

D: Well, the way to do it, after the robbery and all the canceled checks were gone, would be to approach the bank to get photocopies of the checks. The bank never would answer once I told them what I wanted. They never would provide a single photocopy of a single check, and when I went in, my bank officer had been transferred.

W: But basically, if money had been taken out of your account that you didn't take out, you'd've known.

D: No, I was so screwed up I wasn't keeping track. So it's possible there could have been forgeries going through. As a matter of fact, once I began to keep track, I noticed that there were what seemed to me quite large sums missing. Y'see. And I closed my account, notifying the bank, and opened another account; and it was three days later that Barbara noticed that people were gathering outside.

And the bank, although they told me that they had, of course, photocopies of the checks, would never supply them, and never answered the letters after the initial letter when I told them what I wanted. Right, Tess, I couldn't get anything out of the bank?

TESSA DICK: Mm-hm. [Phil's fifth wife, Tessa, was sitting with us or present in the room during most of these conversations.]

D: So you see there are a number of interrelated possibilities: some that involve my ex-wife, some that involve blacks, some that involve the authorities.

W: You suggested in a letter to *Science Fiction Review* that there are Watergate parallels.

D: Yeah. Absolutely. Tess, could you fix me a glass of cold Ovaltine, please?

First of all, the timing of that hit was within a couple of months of the Fielding hit down here, that those strikes occurred within that time segment, in '71. [One of the revelations of the Watergate period was that a White House–linked hit group called "the Plumbers" had broken into the offices of a psychiatrist, Dr. Fielding, looking for material that might damage the reputation of Fielding's patient Daniel Ellsberg, an antiwar activist.] And the M.O. of blowing my files—I saw it on TV, the Fielding files were blown in very much the same manner.

Apparently the first appearance was one of crudeness, as if it had been jimmied by amateurs, using too much force. Only now I understand that that military explosive is a very special kind and consumes itself, and unless you're familiar with it, it just looks like they kind of wrecked it with crowbars. Doesn't look like a blown thing. But I could see the resemblance.

Also, the kind of thing that was taken—papers, documents—is what was taken from the Fielding files, from Dr. Fielding, to try to get incriminating evidence on a person who was a political enemy. There's no doubt that what was primarily sought for in my place was incriminating evidence. There's no doubt about it. In my mind.

W: Is there any reason that the White House or the Justice Department would have taken an interest in you?

D: Umm. This Special Forces guy—it was my only contact ever with a guy who was with Special Forces and also worked with the CIA. Met him in the hospital when I had my shoulder worked on. He didn't know who I was. It was his—after I described how the place was hit, he suggested it might have been the government. He said, "Did it ever occur to you it was the government that did it?" From the M.O. And he said, "What kind of business are you in?" And I said, "I'm a writer." And he says, "Okay, well, what kind of thing do you write?" I says, "Fiction, novels. Science fiction." And he says, "Well, I'll tell you what I would say. I would say your house was hit because you wrote something that was true and you didn't realize it." He says, "Considering it was your files that were hit, papers that were missing, checks, and the kind of explosive and the general condition and the kind of business you were in," he says, "that would be my guess, just without knowing anything about you, and I'd guess that it was the government trying to find out what you knew about something that you had written about fictionally."

W: "Faith of Our Fathers" [a story by PKD about a totalitarian future that appeared in the anthology *Dangerous Visions*].

D: I had been hassled about that by some—well, that's the guess I've always carried in my mind.

But he said to me, "I'll tell you one thing, though, if I'm right"—'cause we had a lot of time in the hospital to sit around and talk about this—he says, "you'll never be able to figure it out, because evidently they didn't find anything to verify this, that you *knew* what you wrote about was true. So you'll never be able to discern which of—" He says, "Have you written very much?" I say, "Oh, yeah, a hell of a lot." He says, "Well, how are you going to know? They obviously didn't find anything; or else if they had you'd have been disappeared fast."

So I could never discern what it might have been, you see? Although we did—he and I discussed several things that he knew about where science fiction might impinge on things that they were working with. Of course the most classic case is the atomic bomb back in the Forties.

W: Yeah, the Cartmill story. [The FBI investigated a story that appeared in a leading science-fiction magazine in 1944 because it described how an atomic reaction could occur—they thought it might represent a breach of security.]

D: He didn't know about that, young guy, but there's an example where I could very easily impinge on something that might be true and I'd have no idea. That might not have anything in it political, you see, something purely abstract in my head that might be a project of some kind. That's the point here. He said, "How in the hell would you ever know, see, if it was fiction?"

W: You weren't doing any other writing?

D: No, none, not the *Free Press,* not a thing.

W: There was no mimeographed stuff coming out of—

D: No. Had no contacts, was on no mailing lists, no memberships, nothing. Clean as a hound's tooth. No. He made a hell of a good point. He says, "With a thing like that, they probably went through that real fast, and could see where you didn't have any knowledge, but," he says, "there's no way you'd know. Thirty-five books or so . . ."

W: In *The Dark-Haired Girl,* the suggestion is also there that Jodie [a young woman PKD was in love with] could have been involved in some way.

D: Yeah. She told me that if I hadn't written a waiver for her, that if she was ever found in my house or in possession of any of my stuff that it was by my permission, that she would have been arrested for the burglary.

W: Why? Because they knew that she hung around there, and was connected to certain people?

D: Well, she told a story that I believed at the time—how true it was I don't know. Her story was that the inspectors came to her and wanted to suborn testimony from her. That they'd gone to all my friends for suborned testimony.

W: What does that mean, exactly?

D: That she would perjure herself, saying I'd committed crimes, in order to send me up, and that if she didn't, they would stick her for the burglary, knowing that she had been in the house and knowing that she was associated with rip-off gangs. It would be easy to hang it on her.

W: So, why—there's another thing, you hadn't mentioned that before, that they were consciously trying to frame you.

D: That's what she said. She said she was a friend of one of the inspectors, which is true, I know she was. She and I had gone into a restaurant together, he was there, she stopped dead, wouldn't go in, and finally she says, "Well, he and I are friends." And later she told me that he'd come to her, that he was trying to get suborned testimony, that they were trying to send me up, they were trying to arrest me. . . .

W: Possibly just because you were hassling them so much, or possibly for some other reason?

D: She said, "They don't understand you, that you're not an evil person." She said, "However, they won't arrest you now," she said, "but you won't get your stuff back." And that's true, they didn't arrest me and I didn't get my stuff back. She also knew that the blacks in the house behind me had been evacuated. She asked if they had moved back. She knew that.

W: You weren't in very much contact with her at this point?

D: Not as much as I had been, no. I didn't know until that moment that she had police contacts. She didn't want me to know. I mean, it was a bummer for her, for her and me to be walking in finding the police inspector there that knew her and knew me. She said, "Well, I don't—he can't say hello to us," and he didn't. She said, "I now have to admit that he regularly comes to me."

It was obvious she was giving him information, and he gave her protection in exchange. She said so. She told me that. She told me that he had proposed that he suborn testimony. She said everybody had agreed to it but her. Which is possibly true and possibly not true.

W: Well, if other people agreed, why didn't they go ahead with it?

D: She said she could break it. And she could. If they didn't get her cooperation.

W: This is also the period of time that [your novel] *A Scanner Darkly* is based on.

D: Yes.

W: A lot of the experience of brain damage, that sort of thing—

D: This covers that. Although it doesn't deal with it all that much, it does deal with it to some extent. It deals with narcotics surveillance, and I'm sure within my circle there was at least one agent provocateur. I know there was. Identified him. And the guy in the house next door was taking license-plate numbers of every car that parked in my place.

D: Well, you see, another kind of people who could be involved in this kind of thing would be the Bureau of Narcotics and Dangerous Drugs. I mean, they have some wild guys that they are kind of only half-involved with, that are like free-lancers for them. But I can't see really the connection of how this—

W: Well, there could be. The cabdriver said, when he looked in the house, he said they were looking for dope. The refrigerator door was hanging open, and outside the attempted points of entry I found heavy-duty polyethylene bags, very heavy-duty, not the kind that we get at the store. And even some food had been put into those polyethylene bags. "I don't know what else you'd find in a refrigerator but dope," I know that's what he was thinking.

[At this point we came to the end of a cassette side, and we used the opportunity to quit for the night. The lightly edited conversation you've just been reading took up forty-five minutes of tape. We returned to the subject of the break-in, with more theories as to who might have done it, and why, later in my visit.]

CHAPTER FOUR

THE THREE NERVOUS BREAKDOWNS

At this point some expanded biographical background might be helpful.

Philip K. Dick was born on December 16, 1928, in Chicago, Illinois. Both of his parents were from Colorado. Phil was born twenty minutes before his twin sister, Jane. The twins were six weeks premature, and Jane died of malnutrition on what would have been their normal delivery date. Phil barely survived. They were born at home, but Phil spent several weeks in the hospital, in an incubator, after Jane's death.

Phil and his parents left Chicago a few months after he was born; they lived in Colorado briefly, then moved to northern California (Alameda, then Berkeley). When Phil was four his father, Joseph Edgar Dick, lost his job, eventually finding another in Nevada. Phil and his mother were to follow him to Nevada, but Phil's mother, Dorothy Kindred Dick, wanted to keep the job she had in the Bay Area, and she requested a divorce. Edgar Dick worked as a bureaucrat (later a consultant and a lobbyist) for the meat industry; Dorothy Dick was an editor for the Children's Bureau, part of the U.S. Department of Labor.

Not long after the divorce, Dorothy was transferred to Washington, D.C. Phil lived there with her from age six to age nine and a half, at which time they moved back to Berkeley.

Dorothy's mother, Meemaw, helped care for Phil during much of his early childhood. He suffered from a variety of illnesses, real and imagined, during childhood, including asthma, tachycardia, and extreme vertigo. Dorothy wrote to Tessa Dick in 1977 that Phil "was so bored at public school—from the beginning—that he didn't work at all and seized every opportunity to stay at home with whatever illness was handy." He went to a boarding school in southern California for a year (eighth grade; ages thirteen to fourteen), then returned to the Berkeley public schools.

As an adolescent, Phil experienced a series of phobias that became so extreme that he stayed home for much of his last year in high school, had a home teacher, and attended regular psychotherapy sessions at Langley-Porter Clinic in San Francisco. He enrolled in the University of California at Berkeley, but attended few classes and soon dropped out altogether.

After Dorothy's younger sister, Marion, died in late 1952, Dorothy married Marion's widowed husband, Joseph Hudner. Phil's cousins Neil and Lynne became his step-brother and stepsister (his only living siblings of any sort).

Phil's great enthusiasm for classical music was well established by the time he was twelve or thirteen; it was probably at twelve that he started reading science fiction. In the summer of 1944, when he was fifteen, he began working for Herb Hollis at University Radio on Shattuck Avenue in Berkeley, and he continued to work there (or at Art Music on Telegraph, a record store also owned by Hollis) until 1952, when he quit the record store to focus full-time on his writing. A year later he was tempted by an offer to manage another music store, but his combination agoraphobia/claustrophobia came back and he had to give it up. So working for Herb Hollis was virtually his only experience in the workaday world; the rest of his life he was self-employed, a full-time writer.

Phil moved out of his mother's house when he turned nineteen, at the end of 1947; a few months later he was married for the first time, to Jeanette Marlin. The marriage lasted about six months.

In 1950 he married his second wife, Kleo Apostolides. They lived together in Berkeley until 1958, when they moved to a remote coastal town in northwest Marin County, Point Reyes Station. Shortly after Kleo and Phil arrived in Point Reyes in the early fall of 1958, they met Anne Rubenstein, a recently widowed woman with three young daughters. This began a romance between Anne and Phil that ended the marriage to Kleo and led to Phil's third and most tempestuous marriage, to Anne R. Dick, in 1959. Anne bore Phil's first child, his daughter Laura Archer Dick, in 1960.

Anne and Phil separated in 1964. Phil moved back to his mother's house in Berkeley and then rented a house in East Oakland (he called it "East Gakville"). By the end of the year, Phil was living with Nancy Hackett, who was to become his fourth wife and the mother of his second child, Isolde Freya Dick. "Isa" was born in 1967.

Nancy and Phil had moved in 1965 from Oakland to San Rafael—Marin County again, but a city rather than a small town. Then in 1968 they bought a house in another part of San Rafael. Nancy and Phil separated in 1970, and it was this house that was broken into in November of 1971.

Phil left San Rafael in January of 1972 to give a talk at a science-fiction convention in Vancouver, British Columbia. It was one of his rare journeys away from California. He apparently had gone on a driving tour of the U.S. with Kleo at some point, getting as far east as Arkansas; he and Anne had driven to Mexico for a day or two to get married in '59; and in 1977 he'd spent a week as guest of honor at a science-fiction convention in Metz, France. I don't know of any other instances where he left California after the age of ten—indeed, it was unusual for him to travel more than a block away from his house or apartment.

In Vancouver he made a serious attempt at suicide, in the wake of which he signed himself into a Synanon-style drug rehabilitation center called X-Kalay. Although heavily dependent on amphetamines, he was not a heroin user like most of the other residents there, and his rationale for being there was that it was the only way he could get constant supervision to prevent another suicide attempt. He was in X-Kalay less than a month, and then flew to Fullerton in Orange County, southern California (about an hour south of L.A., close to Disneyland).

So in 1972 Phil started living in southern California. (He was to spend the remaining ten years of his life in Fullerton and then in nearby Santa Ana.) He chose Fullerton because he had been corresponding with a professor at the state university at Fullerton who wanted Phil's papers to be housed in the university library and suggested to Phil that the Fullerton community would welcome him with open arms.

A few months after his arrival in southern California, Phil, now forty-three, met an eighteen-year-old girl named Leslie ("Tessa") Busby, and they started living together immediately. As soon as his divorce from Nancy was final, he and Tessa were married, and Tessa became the mother of Phil's third child, Christopher (both events occurred in 1973). Phil and Tessa separated in 1976—the occasion of another suicide attempt by Phil.

Phil's mother, Dorothy Hudner, died in 1978. Phil suffered a stroke in his condominium apartment in Santa Ana on

February 18, 1982, and then a more severe stroke in the hospital a few days later. He died on March 2, 1982.

During the interviews in 1974, I brought up a topic that eventually led to Phil's discussing some of the crucial transition times in his life. He did a little dance about it at first, of course. . . .

CONVERSATION, *October 31, 1974*

WILLIAMS: You once said that a great influence on your writing was your own nervous breakdowns—

DICK: I never said that! Where'd I say that?

W: You said it in written responses to the *Double:Bill* questionnaire [a questionnaire sent out to science-fiction writers by an amateur publication in 1963; the responses were published in 1963 and '64].

D: Lies, all lies. They made me say it, invisible forces made me say that.

W: You said that you experienced these nervous breakdowns—

D: I didn't know I said that—

W: —at age nineteen, twenty-four, and thirty-three.

D: I just picked those figures at random, just for—

W: I figure it would be, uh, 1948, right?—which is around the time that you refused to take ROTC.

D: That's about correct, that's approximately right.

W: Which follows what? I mean—

D: You mean which is cause and which is effect?

W: Well, not exactly. I don't think you can make that clear-cut. . . .

D: Could you, uh—

TESSA: Chronological order.

W: Chronological order, right. Can I rephrase the question?

D: [mock menacing voice] Can't you see I'm trying to be evasive, dear? Don't help me when I'm being evasive, I don't need help.

T: He's good at that. He's excellent at being evasive. I say, "Phil, what time is it?" and he says, "Well, um . . ."

D: "Could I have a moment to think?" I say. What I meant was that under undue stress, that I—I bugged out.

W: Well, yeah, that's what it means.

D: All right. Let's be more precise.

W: Then you bugged out. Okay, if that's precise, what the heck do you mean by that?

D: Well, I mean that at about nineteen, um, I was unable to continue doing what I was doing, because I really unconsciously didn't want to do it.

W: Right. And you had to sort of force yourself out of it?

D: Yeah, I couldn't face the fact that I didn't want to do it. I thought I *should* want to do it, and I didn't, so I got phobias and anxieties—

W: And "it" was going to Berkeley and taking ROTC and all that kind of thing?

D: Yeah!

W: Both, right, not just the ROTC?

D: Correct. Yeah, I had a whole bunch of courses that were just so much birdshit, that didn't make any sense at all, and I foresaw in the deep recesses of my mind years and years and years of learning to distinguish one paramecium from another, and then trying to go out in the world and cope with reality on the basis of this kind of jive. But consciously I had been told I had to go to college—

W: You were ahead of your time. That was quite fashionable by the time I got to college.

D: Yeah, I know. Somebody said that to me.

W: We called it "dropping out."

D: Yeah, well, at the time I called it "screwing up."

W: It was heavy even when I did it, but much heavier I'm sure when—

D: You know, I'd been told all my life to go. I was going through high school, you know, getting college-entrance grades, taking a college-prep course, and all that stuff, and everything I did in high school was to get into college.

So I go to college and I'm standing there looking in the microscope. And there aren't even any paramecia in there at all, 'cause the slide moved. And the instruction is, "Draw what you see." And I realize that there's nothing there, nothing at all. But I can't consciously face the fact that this is a symbol of my whole projected four years there, I'm drawing pictures of things that—

W: That aren't even there.

D: So I began to get terribly frightened and anxious and I didn't know why. Now I know why. I would have just screwed my life up forever. My brother, who did do that—stayed in college, went on, got a B.A., then got a master's—is now an usher in a theater. 'Cause he was ill-equipped to do anything. So he's an usher in a theater. That's what he got out of years and years of college. See, he believed it both consciously and un-, or else he suppressed his unconscious, and any questions his unconscious might have had, like, What's the point of all this? You see. He was able to suppress it.

I had too weak an ego to suppress the unconscious pressures. Fortunately I listened to my unconscious because it was too strong to be denied. I was very lucky, I had a powerful unconscious. It drove me out of the academic community, it drove me out of double-domed intellectual pursuits and into—

W: Double-domed?

D: Double-domed. Egghead stuff that I was into. It drove me out of the cloistered realms where I would have been cut off from the broader, truer world, and drove me into the real world. It drove me into a job, and marriage, and a career in writing, and a more substantial life. I found that—

W: Did your first marriage come after that?

D: I'm not through.

W: Oh, I'm sorry.

D: [laughter.]

W: Keep going.

D: I'm very defensive about all this still, you see? Because I didn't finish college. I'm very—am I a bad person?

T: That's okay, I never went.

W: I didn't finish either. I went and I dropped out.

D: God bless you, Paul. I found that I couldn't go into a class and listen to discourses on Locke and Mill and Hobbes, but I could ready the books. And I could also drive all the way across the Rocky Mountains and back and things like that and fix my car and stuff, you know. I carved out a broader reality.

"Dick—the First Breakdown." And I dunno, the second one was when I was married to Anne. I'm not sure—that would've been—wouldn't that be?

W: Um, probably. You dated it here at twenty-four. No, that's earlier, that would be, uh, '53.

D: Oh. I know what that was! Yeah, that's—now there, it's clear as a bell. I had become a writer, and somebody asked me to go back in the record business, offered me the management of a record store, and it was a regular salary, got a very good salary—

W: Very tempting—

D: Yeah, and I felt I should do it because it would give financial security to me and my wife. So I went back in the record business and I immediately got the same phobia that I'd had in the university. I couldn't stand behind the counter, I had to run out of the record store. And, you see, it forced me back into writing again. I was forced to continue writing because I couldn't go back in the record—but I had spent seven years in a record store, seven years behind the counter.

W: So again you couldn't take it, on a conscious level, the

idea that you just really couldn't do it. You thought you were lazy or something.

D: Yeah. See, morally I felt that I ought to hold a regular job, a real job.

W: Were you married at that point?

D: Yeah. Yeah, right. I bought a house, I was married, and I felt I should be leaving in the morning and going to work like everybody else. My unconscious just saturated me with anxiety when I got there, to the record store, and I couldn't comprehend why. And I started to faint.

Now these are obvious conversion symptoms, hysterical conversion symptoms, to get you out of a situation that you don't want to be in. Later I realized, my God, I would have been back in the retail record business, I probably would have abandoned writing. You see what would have happened to me. But I was forced to go back to writing.

W: Right. Isn't it interesting that—and I think this is probably true in a lot of cases—that despite the popular idea, you don't really become a writer and ultimately possibly even a great writer, you don't end up doing it at all because of a terrific high-school teacher or because of great inspiration as a child, but rather because your unconscious mind causes you to flip out when you [laughter] get behind the counter of a record store.

D: Right, right, nothing is left to you but doing that. It's as if Beethoven really wanted to work in the delicatessen, you know, and he got a phobia every time he started to chop up salami, so he had to become a composer.

Now this proves something Jung says, compared to Freud, where Freud would say the unconscious is just a repository of nasty thoughts we don't want to face; and Jung says no, the unconscious is extremely positive and powerful and very often correct, and compensatory to the conscious, and corrects an inadequate conscious view.

Here's a case where a person's conscious view is I should

be a clerk in a record store. Or I should be sitting in a philosophy class learning about Mill and Hobbes. The unconscious says no. And this is not a nasty little repository of sexual things. This is a tremendously powerful teleological thing, looking ahead into the future, driving forward into time.

W: Right. Freud was absolutely brilliant, but he was intimidated, he believed in normalcy.

D: Yeah, right, that he moralized about.

W: And he was afraid of the unconscious.

D: Well, that's the thing, see—these things strike you and they generate great anxiety. Because your conscious attitude is formed along restrictive lines. You know, I'll tell you, the way I've measured it one time recently, your consciousness is built up on introjected moral values that authority figures have deliberately laid on you. Teachers, parents, authority figures have said, "This is right and that is wrong," and this you introject—

W: Especially when you're young.

D: And the unconscious never listens to this stuff, you cannot teach it this way, it will not listen. If it senses a deeper, broader— It's a tremendous spectrum of things, and then there's narrow consciousness, you see, built up by authority figures. The unconscious relates to the entire world, the whole panoply of the universe. It learns from birds, it learns from ads it sees, it learns from television commercials, it learns from everything at once, not just from a few narrow authority figures, parental figures. You see what I mean?

Like, my mother built up my consciousness, my entire world of experience built up my unconsciousness. Now which would you rather go on, your mother or the entire rest of the world? Not just people but everything you see.

W: Dropping out of college must have brought about a lot of conflict with your parents.

D: Ummm—well, they were really indifferent, at that point, but they had instilled those values in my early childhood. It didn't bring up a lot of conflict with them because they weren't prepared to shell out a nickel to put me through college. So in a way it relieved any chance that they might have to shell out anything.

W: What was your father's occupation?

D: He was a lobbyist, in Sacramento.

W: For the state government?

D: To the state government.

W: What sort of thing did he—

D: Cattle. And before that he'd been a federal employee, the Department of Agriculture.

W: So he was a talker? I guess that's what you'd need to do that job—

D: Yeah. Yeah, he—he drove a big Buick and—you know. . . . [Long pause; Phil sounds depressed.] He lost interest in me when I was a baby.

W: Really? What are you, the first, second, third . . . ?

D: Well . . . I'm one-half of twins. My sister, my twin sister, died at about a month old.

W: Really?

D: Yeah.

W: And were you second oldest in the family, apart from the twin?

D: Uh, no, when I refer to other siblings, they're not real siblings, they're fake siblings, they're legal siblings.

W: Different father, or—

D: Different everything.

W: Really?

D: Yes.

W: Why is that?

D: [pause] Tess, would you explain?

T: Well, they were his cousins; but when his uncle's wife died, his mother married his uncle.

D: Morganatic marriage. [He mutters his comments, as though sinking into depression.]

T: In other words, her brother-in-law. After her sister died.

W: Wait. Say that again? His—

T: His mother had a sister who was married and had two kids. The sister died [the tension in the room now is audible, palpable], so Phil's mother married her sister's husband. . . .

W: There's something left out. What about Phil's father?

T: Phil's father had left years before, and they were divorced.

W: This is all still during Phil's childhood—as long as we're talking about him in the third person here?

T: I don't know. He never made that clear.

D: This remarriage was in the Fifties.

W: Oh. Actually then you were raised as an only child?

D: Yes. [long, long pause]

W: I can see you love this subject of conversation.

D: Yeah. [sighs] I was found in a Gladstone bag in South Kensington Station, actually.

W: Is that in Chicago?

D: No, that's in London. That's *The Importance of Being Earnest.* It was all a case of mistaken identity.

W: You grew up in northern California?

D: Yes.

W: Around the Bay Area?

D: Yes. I get very mad when I think about my dead sister.

W: Really?

D: That she died of neglect and starvation. Injury, neglect, and starvation.

W: How do you know?

D: My mother told me. I get very hostile when I think of it. Not toward you—

W: Well, I brought it up.

D: Well, but—that doesn't matter. Anybody that brings it up—uh, I resent the fact that my sister could have lived very readily had she been given normal treatment as a premature baby, as we both were premature. I resent the fact that I would have died too, except for a visiting health nurse—

W: You feel guilty?

D: No, I feel that my mother let her die. And I feel that I

would have—I know I would have died, too, if it hadn't been for a routine inspection by a visiting Cook County health nurse, who happened to notice that both babies were dying and told my mother they had to be taken to the hospital immediately.

But it was too late for my sister. So my mother tells me. How does my mother expect me to feel about that? "Gosh, mom! Jeepers." Something like that? See. I mean, you know, my mother says, "And, oh, we also burned her severely with the hot-water bottle, so it doesn't matter if she died, she would have been crippled anyway."

How am I supposed to feel about that? I mean, you know, I feel very hostile about it, right Tess?

T: Right.

D: See? 'Cause I was a very lonely child, and I would love to have had my sister with me, all these years. But my mother says, "Well, it's just as well she died, she would have been lame anyway, from being burned by us with the hot-water bottle." In which case I suppose— It's like Heinrich Himmler saying, "Well . . . she made a good lampshade, you know, so I guess it worked out all right." You see what I mean?

I never forgave my parents, my m-my parents for negligence like that. It's unforgivable. To me it's still a burning issue. I guess it shouldn't be a burning issue. I wonder why it's a burning issue?

[And then, after some discussion of a related topic . . .]

D: Now . . . [pause]

W: Now?

D: Oh, I'm sorry.

W: When you were thirty-three . . .

D: Well, what year would that have been?

W: That would have been '62. Probably sometime after writing *The Man in the High Castle.*

D: And what happened then?

W: That was your third nervous breakdown.

D: Oh, well, that was my marriage breaking up with Anne. I mean, I was unable to bear the load of the marriage—

W: But your marriage didn't break up with Anne for two more years—

D: Yes, but the realization that I could not carry the responsibilities of the marriage was such that I began to decline under the weight of it. I found myself inadequate to the responsibilities.

W: This was up in Point Reyes.

D: Yes.

W: What specific event did you have in mind when you called that a nervous breakdown?

D: [pause] Ummm . . . the most profound kind of all. I was ceasing to, quote, cope adequately with my responsibilities—

W: As defined by your wife.

D: As defined by my wife. And it was easier to imagine I was having a nervous breakdown than to face the truth about the situation. It wasn't until after I wrote that thing in *Double:Bill*—

W: Which is only a year later, '63—

D: Right. That my psychiatrist told me what the real situation was—which was her psychiatrist, too—that there was nothing wrong with me, that in point of fact the situation was hopeless . . . with her.

W: For you.

D: In other words there was no way I could cope with it, because it was uncopable. It's like some guy, you know, whose car has no motor, trying to start it, and he says—

W: What's wrong with me? I can't start this car.

D: Yeah, what, where did I go wrong? Well, he went wrong 'cause there's no motor in it. I was trying to solve problems that were not solvable. Except by external intervention. I could still be there, and I couldn't solve 'em.

But you could say that I didn't face reality, in that I didn't face the fact that it was not my fault. Which is a kind of strange thing, a strange way of not facing reality, that you could genuinely assume that it's your fault when in fact it's not your fault. That's a weird—that's a weird evasion of reality.

It's like a guy who's got a mine that he's trying to mine something out of and there's nothing in it. And he keeps digging deeper, you know, and saying, "Well, if I just dig ten more feet, I'm sure I'll strike something." It's analogous to that. I kept saying, "If I just try a little harder . . ." It's like the poor guy Charly in, you know, "Flowers for Algernon." He said, "If I'd only tried harder." Remember that? And there was nothing he could have done. That's what's tragic: He kept thinking, If I'd only tried harder.

And in my case I kept thinking, If I only was stronger mentally, psychologically, and everything, to bear these responsibilities. And in point of fact there was no way anybody could stand that situation. No way. It was not an indication of psychological weakness. It was an indication of not facing reality, but a peculiar kind, you see.

But at that time I didn't realize it, I thought I was having a nervous breakdown. As a matter of fact, I was not, in a peculiar way. I was showing the result of terrible pressures on me. . . . It was very hard for me to admit that that marriage could not be saved. Because I loved those children—I had four beautiful children whom I adored. And the only way that marriage could have been broken up would be to leave.

And I did have to leave. And I could not face the fact that I had to leave. Leaving meant leaving those children and never seeing them again. And I left in '64 and I never saw them again. Except for ten minutes, maybe. See? That's ten years, and that's what [voice getting angry]—

W: Did you see Laura during that time?

D: Oh, half an hour.

W: How old is she now?

D: Thirteen. See what I mean? See what that required of me when I left? Anne told me that if I left, I would never see the three older children, the Rubenstein children, again. 'Cause I hadn't adopted them. On the advice of our attorney. 'Cause they were heirs to a very great estate, and if I adopted them they would lose, maybe be cut off from the estate. So I didn't.

She said, "If you leave, you will never see those children again." And that was true. So— And Laura thrown in. Because they were all mixed in together there. And it was true. Her prophecy was true. Now, that was what I had to face if I left. So it was easier to think I could stay there and patch up the marriage. Can you imagine that, leaving those four girls and knowing you'd never see them again? The moment coming when (a) you knew you had to leave, because there was no way to save the marriage, and (b) that this threat would be borne out in fact. And so it was.

I remember what it did to me in '64 when I left. I remember going to Oakland, living in Oakland. There I was, living in this four-bedroom house in Oakland, all by myself, and realizing I'd never see those girls again. Begging Anne to let me see them. Begging their grandparents to let me see them. Getting nowhere. And then the same thing happened again when Nancy left in 1970, taking Isa; she says, you'll never see Isa again. I'm living in a four-bedroom house again. All by myself. Begging somebody to let me see my daughter. It's my karma. Just fucking rotten karma.

W: Laura was your first child?

D: Yeah. She's beautiful. I got a picture of her. That's how I know. I got a photograph of her. A recent one. When she graduated from junior high school or something. She sent me a picture. Tess got her to send it to me. Isn't that something? I know that she's beautiful because I've got a picture of her.

W: She's still living in Point Reyes?

D: Yeah. Laura writes me a lot, though. See, I correspond with her.

W: That's nice. Well, she'll come and see you then, when she's older.

D: Yeah. I've only got to wait four or five more years and then I can see her regularly.

But the other girls are scattered all over the world. Jane got married and she had twins and I sent her some money and a card and she wrote back and didn't include a return address. There's no way I could write to her. Hatte I sent some books to, autographed; she never answered. Tandy, I don't know where she is. That's the price you pay. That's the price I was told I would pay, and I paid it, and it hurt.

W: You had no choice.

D: That's right.

W: The final part of the question is, uh, that you said that this was a big influence on you, these three events, quote, nervous breakdowns, unquote. You said a little more: "Suffering of this sort educates your viewpoint, but at the expense of your creature-comfort principle; it may make you a better writer but the cost is far too great." Well, my question is, assuming that you still agree with that in any way, what—how did it affect your writing?

D: It gave me sympathy for my characters. I could never mock my characters, for screwing up especially. That I was dedicated thereupon to characters who, when walking out the door, would fall over the front step on their nose. And I could never mock 'em for it.

I never felt superior to my characters after screwing up myself. I mean, I took my cow to town and I didn't even get magic beans. I got nothing. And it was my fault, 'cause I was Mr. Stupid. And that gave me a sense of parity with my characters.

Like Jack Isidore [in *Confessions of a Crap Artist*], the world's dumbest person. You know, I could kind of look down on him when I wrote that book, 'cause I was naïve then. That was the Fifties, right? But later on, you see, from Jack

Isidore to Joe Chip [*Ubik*]—I still have a lot of sympathy for Jack Isidore—by the time I'm writing something like Joe Chip, a guy who can't even pay his front door to open, I could no longer see him as a freak.

See, these people are no longer freaks to me, I mean in the sense of being incompetent and fucking up their lives. Because I had completely fucked up my life, I was completely incompetent, and I loved my characters for their incompetence, you see? I could never write down to my characters.

Also it made me need my characters more, as compatriots, friends, cohorts. . . .

CHAPTER FIVE

I think the writer falls in love with his characters, and wants the reader to know of their existence.

—Philip K. Dick, 1976

What matters to me is the writing, the act of manufacturing the novel, because while I am doing it, at that particular moment, I am in the world I'm writing about. It is real to me, completely and utterly. Then, when I'm finished, and have to stop, withdraw from that world forever—that destroys me. The men and women have ceased talking. They no longer move. I'm alone.

I promise myself: I will never write another novel. I will never again imagine people from whom I will eventually be cut off. I tell myself this . . . and, secretly and cautiously, I begin another book.

—Philip K. Dick, 1968

CONVERSATION, *October 31, 1974*

DICK: When I was in Canada, being interviewed on KCLG, the interviewer said to me—he'd never met me before, either—he says, "Listen, you know what I think about you? Let me quote you something F. Scott Fitzgerald said once. Fitzgerald said, 'The characters in my novels are the brothers and sisters I never had.' " He says, "I'll bet you that's true about you, Phil—that they're your brothers and sisters you never had."

Now, can you imagine how that hit? I says, "Yeah, Bob, yeah." And then we talked for a long time about that, although I didn't mention my sister, but—he got it right there, see, he just got it on the spot. That I write about people, and I write from loneliness. And when I write a book, my characters, like Louis Bolero—

WILLIAMS: Leo Bolero.

D: Leo Bolero.

W: Bulero.

D: And what's his name and the other fellow and then those other people, they're all my friends. And then when I'm writing the book, I'm with my friends, and I'm happy. And when I finish the book, I go into a postpartum. They're gone. They walked right out. Doot doot doot doot doot. Down the stairs.

And it just screws my head up, man.

W: How come you've never written a book that's really long? I mean, of the ones you've published, anyway.

D: Fatigue. [pause] Well, for one thing, I don't make adequate notes. After a certain time I start getting confused. I mean, that to carry it in your head, that's about as far as I can carry it.

Now, you know something? I was just thinking. To carry my thought further. To understand what I do. See, I'm doing more than creating the brothers and sisters I never had. They're also the friends I've had. And the friends I might have had. That I am building a universe—this is why, like Ursula said, all my books are really one book. Or something like that. Okay. Now, that's not true, but it is true.

What is true is this. The continuity is that I have built a fantasy world, like little kids do. When I was a little kid, I had a fantasy sister, a make-believe sister, like all kids have make-believe friends. And my novels are my make-believe world, and they're full of my friends. And when I start writing again, I go back into the same make-believe world, sort of.

W: And you're never there.

D: That's true.

W: I mean, as a whole person.

D: That's correct. Because I want to be with them, and I want to have them real.

W: I can't think of any single character in a Phil Dick book who I would say, well, that's Phil. I mean, I could look at Heinlein and say, in *Farnham's Freehold,* Farnham *is* Heinlein. But—

D: If I were given all eternity, I would create an entire universe this way, eventually. Given enough time.

W: With a TV repairman, and a used-car salesman, and a tire regroover, and—

D: Right. And the bosses and their wives and—and I'd slowly build that until we had a town. First we'd have a neighborhood, then a town, then a city, then a county, then a state, then a country, and finally a planet.

And I would never be tired of doing it, I'd—

TESSA: An entire history.

D: Because I would create a race of people. Not idealistic in the usual sense, but to satisfy the needs I have. Which is not an ideal, perfect people, but a people that are real to me. Such as yourself and Tess. People like that. More of the same. But always different, a little. Always the same, but always different.

W: The characters in your books are not based on life. I mean, they're rather based on extrapolation.

D: They're a compo—they're always composites. They're based on life, they're based on extrapolation, they're a synthesis of external people—you know, a number of 'em fused together—but also they are projections of necessities in me, not necessarily components in me, but necessities. These people must be brought into existence, partly from inside out and partly outside observed, and fused together, you see. . . . [pause]

You know, let me tell you a strange thing. That I could do this, for example. It is perfectly conceivable to me that in moments of crisis, I could consult—Louis? Leo?

W: Leo.

D: Leo Bulero, or Runciter, as the Greeks used to consult the Delphic Oracle. [Bulero and Runciter are both business leaders/authority figures who became sympathetic focal characters in *The Three Stigmata of Palmer Eldritch* and *Ubik,* respectively.]

W: How would you do it? I mean, what process would you use to do it?

D: Written form.

W: You'd start writing it, you'd say, uh, "Listen, Leo, I've got a problem here, and I really don't know what to do"?

T: Typing it.

W: Typing it?

D: Yeah. Well, actually, I'd put myself in there, too, in the third person. Um . . . "He walked into the office. 'Glen,' he said to Runciter, 'could I have a few minutes of your time? I've got a problem here I can't handle.' Runciter glanced up." And then so on. And . . . "Glen, the problem is as follows. What do you think I should do?" And actually I could gain from Runciter's responses things that I could never extract from any other—

W: Runciter would say, "You're full of shit, don't take up my time with this kind of thing." Then he'd tell you his problems.

D: I wouldn't know till I wrote it. But the point is that

Runciter would say something that I would never think of. Just like a good ventriloquist, where the dummy talks and says things he would never say.

W: Like a way of talking with ourselves?

D: That's true, it's a colloquy. You know, it shows a lot of what we do in real life is talking to the dialogue within ourselves anyway. We listen to the psychiatrist, we listen to somebody whom we respect, and yet, in a way, part of it's projected from ourselves.

T: And we discard anything that we wouldn't say ourselves.

D: This whole thing is a very strange business, that like just having done this screenplay [when I visited, Phil had recently finished writing a screenplay based on his novel *Ubik*—his first and only screenplay—on assignment from a French director, Jean-Pierre Gorin], Runciter and Joe Chip became so real to me that I can imagine writing about them forever. And they'd always say new things, you know. But they would evolve, I imagine, under those circumstances. And I could learn from what they said.

Okay, where was this wisdom before I wrote it down? Was it in my head? No, it really wasn't. Didn't take place until it's the deed, as Faust said, Goethe's Faust said. He said, "In the beginning was the word? In the beginning was the deed." Well, this occurs in the deed, the act of writing. These things occur when you write, not in thinking.

W: I don't write characters or dialogue, yet I have the same thing. If I really get going on a piece of writing where I essentially am thinking or I'm talking to the reader or with the reader, then I will say things—I mean I will invariably say things that I never thought of.

D: So you have the same experience?

W: I think probably a lot of writers or musicians or people like that do, in different ways, and to different degrees. Maybe part of it is how much you're willing to go with that experience, too. I mean, some people might—their characters might start talking to themselves and the author would say, "Shut up! I'm in charge here!"

D: I had a funny experience I'd never had before, in that regard. Before I did the screenplay, before I knew I was going to be doing the screenplay, before Jean-Pierre wrote to me, I had these dreams that—in which I was somebody else. I know I wasn't myself.

For one thing, I went in the kitchen and talked to my mother and it wasn't my mother, it was somebody else entirely. I noticed that when I got out my wallet, I had a great deal of money, and the bills were arranged differently than I arrange them. And I began to grasp the fact that my friends were a different set of people. And when I woke up, I thought, "That's strange, I was inside that person looking out." I mean I had a sense of identity, but . . .

And then later when I was doing the screenplay, I discovered scenes in the novel which I had dreamed. And I was dreaming from the standpoint of some of the characters in the novel. For instance, I dreamed that scene in the book where Al Hammond takes out—well, let's put it the other way.

I dreamed that I was taking out my wallet and giving some money to a kind of a nitwit guy who had to take a drive to go to a funeral. And I was giving him some bills. And I'm reading *Ubik,* and there's this scene where Al Hammond gets out his wallet and gives Joe Chip some money, to pay for a hotel bill, and then of course Runciter's dead, and the funeral is coming up soon. . . . The similarity was too great to ignore. But I hadn't read *Ubik* for years, and I didn't know at the time I had the dream that I was going to be doing the screenplay. And I find that very strange.

Now of course when I wrote the screenplay it made it very easy for me to write those scenes, because I had already been through . . . I found in fact dream after dream that I had were scenes from *Ubik.* But it makes me wonder, you know, are these characters really real? Do I think I invent them, but in actual fact I am merely picking them up from somewhere?

W: Well, in some sense they're real. I mean, we don't have to go very deeply into that to say that there's some level on which they are real. Not necessarily as flesh, but, uh—

D: Well, I had the strange feeling that somehow this had really happened, somehow, in some way, as I did the screenplay; that I was describing things that actually had happened.

W: Like a medium.

D: Yeah. Exactly. But I couldn't explain that feeling. I just couldn't give an explanation of it. But, um—well, I remember one dream I had.

In the dream Tess and I were in the kitchen on a high stool. We'd found a cereal box, and on the back of the cereal box is extremely valuable information, directed at us. And we were both reading it. And the relationship between that and *Ubik* is an obvious one. [In *Ubik* Joe Chip is constantly getting personal messages from his dead boss, Glen Runciter; for example, on a matchbook cover.] The ads were directed at Joe Chip. And that's precisely what I dreamed. And this kind of dream continued for months, where written information like that was directed at me. Although they weren't perhaps as conspicuously like *Ubik* as the cereal-box one.

W: Well, I'm sure that many of us have had that feeling in the daytime. I mean, you walk down the street and you see a poster that relates to—in some completely different sense than it was intended—to what you're supposed to do today.

D: Exactly! Now if I'd known I was going to be doing a screenplay of *Ubik,* or was in process, but at that point I had no idea I'd ever be going over *Ubik.* And yet here I am dreaming scenes from *Ubik,* obviously related to *Ubik,* to the basic experience in *Ubik* of being addressed through cereal boxes and things like that. But I can't account for that.

Except that I am absolutely sure that in *Ubik* I touched upon, as Lem says [Stanislaw Lem, noted Polish novelist and critic, who has written extensively about Dick's work], touched upon something that is real but we've lost track of it. He said, "resurrected a sacerdotal power," something like that, "that has been buried for aeons." In that book, somehow. But what he means by that I don't know. I do not know what he means.

W: What, uh—you said in a letter to me that you found out that *Ubik* was really true.

D: Did I tell you that?

W: Uh . . . [reads] "Did you know that *Ubik* is true, and we're in a sort of cave, like Plato said, and they're showing us endless funky films? And now and then reality breaks through, as in *Ubik,* from our friend who was here once and then died, but has turned back."

D: Well, yeah, that puts it beautifully. That shows how much better I can write than I can talk. Isn't that funny? I could never say that.

In 1971 Patrice Duvic, from Editions Opta, came over to see me, and he was talking about *Ubik.* And at one point, which I think was later, actually '72, he said, "Phil, *Ubik* is one of the five most important books ever written." And I—I asked him to explain. "Five most important science-fiction novels?" "No, no." "Five most important novels?" "No, no." "Five most important books ever written?" "Yes." "In what way?"

Now, he couldn't tell me, but he talked something about a new view of the Platonic forms, the archetypal forms. But he was unable to explain. Which is a shame. I would love to have . . . Okay. Then I read Lem's article. Lem spoke almost the same way. And then a guy comes over from France, another guy, that didn't know Duvic, and he says that—these guys said very similar things, you see, but they never were able to explain it. Okay. But, I mean, there was enough people saying that to make *Ubik* the most highly esteemed American science-fiction novel in France, I was told, see.

W: Apparently, yeah.

D: And also in Poland, and in Pocatello, Idaho.

W: No, I don't believe in Pocatello, Idaho.

D: Oh, you've got to do that, because this girl is writing a thesis on me and she lives there, and she said she went to the bar on Lomack Street to get a drink, and the bartender was reading *Ubik.*

W: Somebody was reading a science-fiction book at the front desk at a building a friend of mine manages, a dormitory for medical students, and like twelve people stopped by the desk in the next hour and said, "Oh, you're reading a Phil Dick book," and wanted to start conversations about it.

D: [muttering] It's the end of the world. . . . This was prophesied in Revelation, along with the nine-headed beast. . . .

This theme of the relationship between an author and the people and worlds he creates was also touched on in a conversation a day earlier, October 30, 1974. We had been talking of Phil's interest in the multicharactered realistic novels produced by students in the French department of Tokyo University after World War II.

D: What fascinated me was the economy of it, same structure [as the French realistic novels], but sparse. That's what I used in *The Man in the High Castle.*

W: Where you start off with one character, and then, in the next chapter, introduce a new character and set them in motion towards each other, that sort of thing?

D: Right. And then if you'll draw a diagram, you'll find that Childan is the first character, knows Tagomi, and ultimately they're all linked, but you can't say that any one character knows all the other characters. I once diagramed it.

W: And you never brought them all together in one room.

D: No, 'cause I thought that was dumb. That was like, towards the end of this Japanese novel's structure, the grotesque scenes required to bring all of them together, it became most of the work was spent figuring out how to get 'em all together.

What this all seems to me to be, looking back on why I was drawn to it, why I really didn't think much of the conventional novel structure, English/American, was that, well, first of all, the idea of a single protagonist. I never could understand that too well. But that's been forced on me, finally, that you have the viewpoint character that must subsume all the others, really, um, I guess [his voice gets squeaky], usually you gotta do that, but the thing that I've felt, Paul, is that problems are multipersonal, they involve us all, there's no such thing as a private problem.

W: I like that. I think that in all of your books, they're really group problems, you know, the way people's problems tend to rub off on each other is very interesting.

D: Right. Well, the other thing is the medieval idea that what is true in heaven is true on earth. I mean, all the levels of the universe are the same thing, or synchronicity. That's how the *I Ching* works, right?—that the macrocosmos and the microcosmos have synchronous similarities.

That, um, it's only a form of ignorance, when I wake up in the morning and I fall over the chair and break my nose, and I'm broke, and my wife's left me—it's my ignorance that makes me think I'm an entire universe, and that these miseries are my own and that they're not affecting the rest of the world.

If I could only look down from a satellite, I would see all the world, everybody, getting up, to some extent, in some analogous way, falling over a chair, and breaking something.

This is a—that we are all caught up in a common destiny, right? That it's not identical, but it has some kind of parallelism amongst it. We're all linked, our destinies are linked—that's how I feel.

I really think that maybe the first responsibility of the novelist, as I conceive it, is to show this. He starts with a character and surmounts the view the individual reader has that he is a world unto himself, nobody else shares his problems and he doesn't share theirs.

Then switch to another character and show some involvement. But the way they're involved is difficult to define—I mean, you can't really say that everybody has bad luck the same day, or that we're all, you know, comrades at the barricades. It isn't like that; it's that somehow we are linked, and maybe that's it, that the real thrill of the writing is to work through sixty thousand words without a preconception as to how these characters are linked.

I don't go into these things with . . . For *Man in the High Castle* I had a little tiny piece of paper with the names of a couple of characters on it, and the general idea that the Germans and Japanese had won the war. That's all I had. That in starting the book I was investigating for myself the links between people, what were the common qualities, the ubiquities of their existence.

You know, writing the book I don't have a preconception. It emerges. I learn as I write. . . .

W: That's what I've felt, from reading the books. It's really fascinating, because they sort of happen—

D: They are a happening, man. I make use of what's called "happy accidents"—my whole books are happy accidents. [to Tessa] What's that you took out?

T: That's your notes on your novel.

D: Oh. I'm writing a sequel to *The Man in the High Castle.* [*High Castle,* published in 1962, is one of Dick's best-known novels; it won the Hugo Award for Best Science-Fiction Novel of the Year. The book takes place in an alternate universe where the Germans and Japanese won World War II and jointly occupy the United States. The "man in the high castle" is a mysterious author named Hawthorne Abendsen, actually a minor character in the book, who has written a novel widely circulated in the underground about a world in which the Allies won the war. Abendsen's book is called *The Grasshopper Lies Heavy.*]

D: [resumes his train of thought after some fooling around with the tape recorder] There is something else that precedes sitting down at the typewriter, and that is a—a—a scent of the reality of the characters. They are there, the major ones. And I gradually discern their world, starting from them. You know what I mean? First I perceive the—

Okay, the best thing to do, maybe, in this, is the sequel to *Man in the High Castle,* since I have not started writing it. Let's look at what I can discern now, because here I'm really stuck with the proof of what I'm saying—how much I really know now. 'Cause I was about to start typing when I dislocated my shoulder. I would normally be ready to go to the keyboard.

All I know is, it picks up with Hawthorne Abendsen, that's all I—I see him—

W: 'Cause he played a very small role in the first book.

D: Right, in other words he just came in at the end. And I see him, he's in that house that we saw at the end, but he's all alone. I sound like a, you know, a medium, talking about—

W: He's in the house, right, and—

D: And the letter is under the flowerpot. But I really see it in my— When I was doing the screenplay, I realized I've got a little screen in my head, and the people walk around on it.

W: They're real.

D: They're little, Paul, they're about that big. [laughter]

Yeah, they move around, you know, and I was going like this, looking up, talking and saying, "and there goes Joe out the door, slam!" You see?

W: Heinlein is definitely one writer who that must also be true for. You can really see that in his books. In fact, he said that, that the stories write themselves, in a way; he's always fascinated to see what's going to happen.

D: Yeah. Yeah. I didn't realize it until I did the screenplay, where I had to visualize, and I realized I didn't have to 'cause that was—I didn't know any other way to do it. And I got to going—I was literally looking up, type type type and look up. "Okay, now, there's Hawthorne Abendsen. And he's alone in the house. The wife is gone. And there was a child, 'cause we saw a tricycle in the driveway. So the wife and the child are gone."

It shows how little I impose on my characters. I deduce he has a child 'cause of the tricycle. And it's later, because time must have passed, they couldn't have left in a minute or two.

Now I've recorded about ten spools of tape, on a theoretical thing. But you can't write a theoretical thing, because we're talking here about dramatic fiction. [Having listened to some of his tapes, I believe what he means is that he has recorded notes for the book, but they're not notes on plot or characters, primarily; they're more conceptual background, like speculating on what has really happened to this character, and why. Thus, "theoretical." I would guess that he was recording because his shoulder was out and he couldn't write. Later he began writing down his "notes for the new novel," actually notes about what happened to him in February and March of 1974, which had become the thematic basis of the planned novel. These are the notes that eventually ran to well over a million words—possibly 2 million—and are called, by Phil, his Exegesis.]

The sequel's called *Valisystem A,* which stands for Vast Active Living Intelligence System A, which is like, you know, an artificial intelligence, AI system. That, um— uh— [whispering] God, I can't remember a goddamn thing about it.

Which just goes to show you exactly what I'm talking about. I can see him there, and I know what the book is about, that it's about a, uh—Tess! Do you remember anything about *Valisystem?* Doing the screenplay wiped out the— Do you remember what it was about, at all? Can you give me any clues?

T: Well, it's this AI system that Abendsen is in contact with.

D: Why? What happens? Do you remember any plot?

T: Well, it—it actually wrote *The Grasshopper Lies Heavy,* and it wants him now to do another book.

D: And what is the book about? Now he knows about its existence, he knows about Valisystem A.

T: It's about, uh, I think it's about the—jeez, I think about what happened to Abendsen after *The Grasshopper Lies Heavy.*

D: Well, okay, it wrote—that's where he got *The Grasshopper Lies Heavy.* It's not from the *I Ching,* then—well, of course it's not from the *I Ching.* It can't really write a book.

W: Uh, is Julia in it?

D: [pause] No! Guess not. She ain't there. She's gone. Oh . . . The Nazis got him. Remember? That's what was happening in *The Man in the High Castle.* They were trying to assassinate him.

And Juliana got him. She got the assassin. And Abendsen sort of sat there and smiled a lot and talked, talked highfaluting talk at the end of the book. Yeah. But when this [book] begins, he has been zapped by 'em. His house is in ruins. His wife and child are dead. No wonder I can't remember it. I mean, I've got almost a block against it.

And he—it's later, it's a couple of years later, and he has been—they got him, they got him, man, they really super got him, they got his wife, they killed his wife, they killed his son, they destroyed all his records and notes and everything and put him out of business, and what he's living in is like a bombed-out cellar in World War One.

This just shows, the hand of tyranny done reached out, just as it began to in *The Man in the High Castle.* Part of this is a flashback, in that his memory is defective as to what happened to him. That is, he's nuts, sort of, lying there in the rubble, living on still, not too sure of what happened, and certainly defeated as an antagonist to the tyranny. There is nothing he can do.

He's been terrorized into almost a kind of senility. Like a wino, where he's no longer conscious of space and time, in a kind of an endless haze. And with a Nazi agent provocateur hanging around him all the time, too, now—instead of just on his way to Abendsen, an agent provocateur is there, as his companion, his friend, and his jailer. Feeding him drugs, giving him enough money to live on, reading anything that Abendsen writes. So he's a prisoner in the ruins of his own house. Not killed, but so damaged that he's no longer a danger. And trying to reconstruct what happened to him. How'd he get from there, with his wife and child and his intact home and everything, to this? You see? He's trying to remember. And also, what can he do?

He finds himself contacted—I'm giving you the whole plot in a sentence, and if you put it in the interview . . . you cost me my career [laughs crazily, like Mozart in the film *Amadeus*].

Here's how it comes out. He finds himself contacted by a sentient entity, a living force, which is chameleonlike enough to evade even his detection of where it is, who it is, where it comes from.

It manages to slip past his captors, with all their technological gadgets and all their vigilance, in the most elusive ways imaginable. . . . Much more elusive than Runciter, contacting Joe Chip through matchcovers and things like that. Those at least you could show around. You could show somebody a matchcover on which there was a message. This escapes almost as fast as he sees it; it's almost as if it is temporary arrangements of things which when someone else looks have already vanished.

W: It really makes him wonder about himself.

D: Of course. And in mentioning it to his captor, who plays a dual role—you remember O'Brien in *1984,* who was his friend and also his tormentor later? But in this case, the guy's both friend and tormentor simultaneously.

In a strange way—I mean, it's *impossible* to deduce what this Nazi is doing, he's so polymorphous. And this appears to be another aspect of Abendsen's derangement, his sense of the presence of something; and yet it is gradually reshaping him into a potent force against the tyranny. But in so elusive and indirect a way that even he, if he were interrogated under Pentothal, could not tell that.

In fact, we've got scenes where you switch viewpoints, they've got him under drugs, and they're saying, "Herr Abendsen, you seem to be writing again. What are you writing?"

And he says, "I don't know."

"Well, where are you getting these ideas?"

"I don't know."

"Who is giving them to you?"

"I don't know."

"Well, they must come from somewhere."

"Yeah, I guess they must."

It's like Solzhenitsyn writing in the Soviet Union. They can look over everything he's written, and examine it, and they can try to find out the source, and so on.

That's Valisystem, Vast Active Living Intelligence, he calls it that. That's what he arbitrarily assigns it, since it never identifies itself.

Now, you see, that's all I have to go on.

W: Right.

D: And, um, it's a—it's—it's—I don't know if you—would you call it—you can't exactly call it a plot idea.

W: Well, it's the beginning of—

D: It's a—it's—

W: Yeah, it's a plot idea. I mean, it's not what anyone else would do, you know, it's different.

D: Is that right?

W: I guess.

D: I guess . . . To epitomize it in the abstract, to extrapolate, it is the story of someone who has been destroyed, who is helpless and friendless. Someone comes to his rescue, and this is a study of someone who is never glimpsed clearly but who is there to help him.

W: Right. Well, we know that, we do have the given, from the last book, of the tyranny, so we know what the outside force is, in effect, that he's coming up against, although there's no telling what else he's gonna come up against in the course of this thing.

D: You mean his antagonist?

W: Yeah.

D: Oh, yeah, there's no doubt about what he's pitted against. Also there's no doubt of what destroyed him. He may not remember very well, but we can assume.

W: I would guess that geographically there's no telling what kind of ground he may end up covering in this book.

D: The main thing is that it will center around Abendsen, which the other book was deficient in that it didn't center around Abendsen. And also, how does one fashion a book of resistance, a book of truth in an empire of falsehood, or a book of rectitude in an empire of vicious lies? How does one do this right in front of the enemy?

Not through the old-fashioned ways of writing while you're in the bathroom, but how does one do that in a truly future technological state? Is it possible for freedom and independence to arise in new ways under new conditions? That is, will new tyrannies abolish these protests? Or will there be new responses by the spirit that we can't anticipate? Will it be equally new? We can't really . . .

See, I can't do it in advance of writing it. If I could tell it, I would—

W: Yeah, you wouldn't be able to write it.

D: Probably. But I feel him there, confused, injured, and in shock, drawing his horses together and trying to resume the stance that he had, which was to pit himself against the tyranny. But now things seem to be worse.

But on the other hand he's not alone, perhaps. Although he can never be . . . Now that's another thing. *He* can never be sure if this Valisystem is real. The real question for the plot would not be whether the Nazis could determine if he was receiving some kind of elusive assistance, but whether he could determine if it was real. You know what I mean? Or if he was, in a sense, imagining that someone was giving him assistance.

But if it was helping him, what would the criterion be? I mean, you know, if he only dreamed that he heard a voice telling him what to do, how to do it, this is a phantasm of his own mind. And yet, if the results are the same . . . It raises . . . Oddly enough, Paul, you'll be amazed to discover that I tend to want to treat the questionness of what is real.

W: [laughs]

D: Only instead of it being a question of what is real externally, it now invades the inner psyche.

Is this real, this assistance, because it's— That's why I'm— There I go, I've got my old problem again, don't I? I never—

W: Yeah. But it takes a lot of different forms. I mean, it's not like— there's no repe— I mean, there's lots of repeating of names and themes and all that sort of thing, but I don't think there's any real repetition in any of your books.

D: Well, thanks. Terry Carr said . . . [Phil loved to talk about how science-fiction editor Terry Carr told him all his books were exactly the same, and that it was time for him to stop pussyfooting around and say what is real and get on with it.]

You know, Paul, I hadn't realized until that moment, it's the same preoccupation with what is real, that try as I can, if I sat down to write a story about a zebra, and that it wanted to get into the zoo so people would admire it, it would wind up with it asking itself if zoos are real, or something like that. There's always this . . .

I'm really not pleased to discover that I'm back at my same—

W: Well, what I was going to say is, Terry Carr is wrong, because although you can reduce it for descriptive purposes, to saying, "It's about what is real," that's deceptive, because all that says is that that's a very broad theme, or that's a very encompassing description.

D: It's like saying that he paints human figures, the artist paints human figures.

W: It's more like saying that the novelist's entire body of work can be seen as the exploration of what is real, in other words an exploration of reality. A much bigger canvas—

D: The thing that strikes me is that I've cut myself off a really different version of this, then, because I thought I had ended this problem. And it just came around from behind much worse. Because the way I was always phrasing it was in terms of *a posteriori* knowledge—that is, empirical knowledge, which is all sophisticated versions of, you know, "Is this chair real?" It's that sort of simplistic philosophical thing, it's sort of a kind of solipsism.

This is a little different, because this entity never appears tangible to him, in the sense that we see something that appears tangible and is really cardboard and they only put it there to fool us.

Those are like paranoia—they built a set around us, and we believe that set is real, because we've been programmed to believe it's real.

W: Right. Anyway that's the simplest—*Time out of Joint* is like the simplest example of—

D: Crude, crude. And this, here, is a really difficult form, because what seems to be real to him is never visible at all, and never tangible, and yet he deduces its existence by its effects.

Which is a very Beckett-like thing, isn't it? You know, where Beckett—remember that thing where Beckett saw people as planets, rotating around him? Because he only knew them by the time they came, that some people, one particular person, would come at ten in the morning, and he deduced the qualities of that person by the time that person arrived. So it was finally a kind of cosmology, a solar system of people.

And in this case it's partially within him, partially outside and partially within, which a chair is never located in such a complex way. He's confronted by it in privacy, as an inner experience. But he's also confronted with it as an outer experience. And of course he then immediately thinks, Am I projecting an inner experience, or am I introjecting an external experience? But it is no longer localized, in a simple empirical way. The boundaries of what is me and what is not me are now examined on a wholly different basis.

[Phil never did write the sequel to *The Man in the High Castle* that he just described for us. He took notes for two years, then wrote a very different version of *Valisystem A* in the summer of 1976 (published posthumously in 1985 as *Radio Free Albemuth*), took notes for two more years, and wrote another very different book called *Valis* in fall 1978 (published 1981). All the books from this period, including the unwritten ones, are consciously autobiographical.]

CHAPTER SIX

DYING IN THE GUTTER

Though I wrote the Gospels in this century, I should die in the gutter.

—Herman Melville, circa 1851 (while writing *Moby Dick*)

I hate to say it, Phil, but unmistakably you're pushing "mainstream" talent through the narrow channels of sf. In a way, maybe you're right to do so, because some of the jewelry in your things would have to be plated over to be popular out there. Maybe you're too good for mainstream, because the poor term has come to signify both "really good writing" and Book-of-the-Month-Club appeal. And the really good writing has just as small an audience in general lit. as anywhere. In some ways—sorry about all these qualifiers—your situation reminds me of Vonnegut's, except that you haven't his flaws and you have much more to say, far greater depths. I incline to think he has made it mainstream because of his flaws. It's a goddam shame those idiots out there won't find you, but I bet their unborn kids will. And maybe I'm a lousy prophet and the lightning has already struck.

—James Tiptree, Jr., in a letter to Philip K. Dick, 1969

> I made my first sale in November of 1951 and my first stories were published in 1952. At the time I graduated from high school I was writing regularly, one novel after another. None of which, of course, sold. I was living in Berkeley and all the milieu-reinforcement there was for the literary stuff. I knew all kinds of people who were doing literary-type novels. And I knew some of the very fine avant-garde poets in the Bay Area, Robert Duncan and Jack Spicer, Philip Lamantia, that whole crowd. They all encouraged me to write, but there was no encouragement to write science fiction, and no encouragement to sell anything. But I wanted to write and sell. And I also wanted to do science fiction. My ultimate dream was to be able to do both literary stuff and science fiction.
>
> Well, it didn't work out that way.
>
> —Philip K. Dick, interview with John Boonstra, 1981

At the time of his death, Philip K. Dick could look back on two writing careers, one of which had been, despite a great many low points, extraordinarily successful; and the other of which seemed to have been an almost total failure.

He was not the most popular science-fiction writer of his day (in France, perhaps, but not in the U.S., where in sales appeal he wasn't even in the top twenty), but he was regarded by a great many writers and critics as the finest science-fiction writer in the world. His most experimental science-fiction novel yet, *Valis,* perhaps the world's first metaphysical picaresque novel, was not only getting fine reviews but also selling much better than anyone had expected. Income from overseas sales and movie deals had put his earnings above $100,000 a year for at least the past three years. He had dozens of works in print constantly, in the U.S. and a score of other countries, and a major film based on one of his books was about to be released.

Best of all, he was receiving continual confirmation, in the form of critical essays, comments by peers, and letters from readers, that his science fiction was in fact achieving the depth and intensity and range of effect on readers that he aspired to and worked for. As he lay paralyzed and waiting for death after his crippling stroke in February 1982, Phil could feel satisfied that his career as a science-fiction writer had been a glorious success.

Phil's other career, that of literary or mainstream writer, had been a sour one of endless disappointments, but at least it ended on a strikingly positive note. Philip K. Dick wrote more than a dozen mainstream novels between 1951 and 1960, and actually quit writing science fiction altogether for several years in an effort to get his stalled literary career off the ground. But none of those novels were ever published (nor were the literary short stories that he said preceded them) until a small press produced a limited edition of his 1959 mainstream masterpiece *Confessions of a Crap Artist* in 1975. ("When *Confessions* appeared," he told Charles Platt in a 1979 interview, "that took the sting out of it, and I didn't feel so bad.")

But as Phil lay dying he had the satisfaction of knowing he had just sold a new mainstream novel to a major publisher for the first time in his career, and that it was to appear in hardcover in the spring of 1982. And although like most writers he had flurries of doubt about everything he'd ever written, I think he died also knowing the new novel, *The Transmigration of Timothy Archer,* was marvelous, a major work.

In the end, of course, both of Phil's careers are one, and as the processes of time and taste select the works of his that belong in the permanent literature of humankind, they will not be placed in two segregated piles, "mainstream" and "science fiction." But the pain of that distinction, and of his ability to play in only one of his two chosen playgrounds, was very real for Phil throughout his lifetime as a professional writer.

Phil Dick first came to the attention of the science-fiction world as an extraordinarily prolific short-story writer. His first stories were sold in 1951 and appeared in print in 1952. By May of 1953 he had stories in seven different magazines in the same month, all science-fiction or fantasy magazines; in all, he had thirty stories published in 1953. Some were outstanding, some were mediocre; many of them held at least hints of the themes and interests that were to dominate Dick's fiction throughout his career.

In 1955 Phil Dick's first books appeared: a novel, *Solar Lottery,* and a collection of short stories (published in Britain only), *A Handful of Darkness.* Two more novels *(The World Jones Made* and *The Man Who Japed)* appeared in 1956, and two more *(Eye in the Sky* and *The Cosmic Puppets),* plus another collection of stories *(The Variable Man),* in 1957.

Phil had a pat story about why he started writing novels—by the time he related it to me it was like a parody of his own story: "In '54 I went to my first convention. And they said, 'You oughta write novels! You'll never make it writing stories.' [Because the financial return was so small; novels brought in more income for the time and effort involved.] So I says, 'Oh? Is that how you do it?' And they say, 'Yeah. Have a martini.' And I say, 'What's a martini?' "

In fact Phil had already completed *Solar Lottery* before he went to that convention. And he had written a fantasy novel earlier, *The Cosmic Puppets,* but he thought of it as a long story and his agent was trying to sell it to the magazine market. It finally appeared in a magazine in 1956, and as a result was picked up for book publication in 1957, so it seemed to have been written later than it actually was.

But Phil's awareness of himself as a science-fiction novelist began when *Solar Lottery* was sold at the end of 1954, and it had a dramatic effect on his short-story production. In just over three years, from November '51 to the end of '54, Phil Dick had written eighty-two short stories. In the next eight years, 1955–62, Phil wrote exactly four stories, two in

'55 and two in '58. When he made the decision to change forms, he didn't look back.

Another momentous decision followed in 1956: Phil stopped writing science fiction altogether. Since before 1951, before Phil met Tony Boucher, editor of *The Magazine of Fantasy and Science Fiction,* in the record store where Phil worked, and started attending Tony's writing class—which led to Phil's first sale, when Tony bought his story "Roog"—before all that, Phil had been writing literary or mainstream novels, and he never stopped writing them and trying to sell them, no matter how busy he got with the science fiction.

Phil had a respected agent who worked energetically to market what Phil called his "straight novels." They were seen by scores of publishers, treated respectfully, considered seriously. Some of them came very close to being bought. Then in 1956 Phil apparently decided that what he needed to be successful was to focus all his energies on his mainstream work. At any rate, despite a growing reputation and a receptive marketplace, Phil wrote no science fiction at all in 1956 and 1957.

Unfortunately, his straight novels—both the ones already written and the new ones he turned out during 1956–57—still couldn't find a publisher.

In 1958 Phil made a sort of breakthrough: He wrote a novel that is realistic and related in style, tone, and content to his mainstream novels for the first four-fifths or so, and then the growing tension of small details adding up, suggesting that the world of the characters is not what it seems, breaks into a full-fledged science-fictional situation for the last fifth of the book. And he sold this novel, *Time out of Joint,* to "a major US hardcover publisher" (as he wrote in a letter at the time), Lippincott, who brought it out in 1959 not as science fiction but as "a novel of menace."

Was this the escape from the science-fiction ghetto? It could have been, I suppose, but nothing much happened. Lippincott couldn't even find a paperback publisher to sell the rights to. Phil's advance was $750, less than he had been getting from Ace Books for the paperback Dick novels they'd already published.

In 1959 Phil wrote the finest, most mature mainstream novel of his early period, *Confessions of a Crap Artist.* It came painfully close to being accepted by several of the most respected literary publishing houses in New York. One publisher even gave Phil a contract and a cash advance on his next, unwritten, mainstream novel, as an expression of their enthusiasm for his work, their certainty that he was just on the edge of doing something not only publishable but exceptional.

Spurred by this (but unable, presumably because of his phobias, to visit New York as the publisher urgently requested), Phil wrote two more straight novels in 1960, and then, when they also failed to sell, realized it was time to give up writing altogether.

(He had also done some science-fiction work in 1959–60, of a particularly demeaning sort: because he needed money, he rewrote and expanded two very early [1953] and sloppy novelettes into novels for Ace Books—*Dr. Futurity* and *Vulcan's Hammer.* Why didn't he write any new sf? There are indications that in addition to wanting to focus his energies on his literary efforts, he was also depressed about the state of the science-fiction market; it was at a low ebb at the end of the Fifties, in terms of the size of the audience and the number of magazines and publishers to sell to, whereas it had been at a high point when Phil first entered the field.)

So at the end of 1960, his hopes of literary success dashed after years of perseverance, Phil took stock of his situation—he had an infant daughter and three step-daughters to support—and decided that he had better put away his typewriter and go to work helping his wife, Anne, with her jewelry-making business.

* * *

This would be the end of our story, except for the intervention of the hand of fate in the form of excruciating boredom.

"I wasn't happy. I didn't enjoy making jewelry. I had no talent whatsoever. My wife had the talent. I couldn't do anything except polish what she made." (PKD to John Boonstra, 1981.)

"I decided to pretend I was writing a book. To make the fabrication convincing, I actually had to start typing. I had no notes, I had nothing in mind, except for years I had wanted to write about [a world in which] Germany and Japan had beaten the United States. And without any notes, I sat down and began to write, simply to get out of the jewelry business." (PKD to Daniel DePrez, 1976.)

The book was *The Man in the High Castle.* It was completed in November 1961. "When I had the manuscript finished I showed it to her [his wife, Anne]. She said, 'It's all right, but you'll never make more than $750 off of it. I don't even see where it's worth your while to submit it to your agent.'" (Boonstra interview, 1981.)

Phil did send the book to his agent, and it sold immediately to a prestigious publisher, Putnam, who brought it out in hardcover in late summer 1962. Again, it was not published as science fiction; instead, the cover blurb says, "An electrifying novel of our world as it might have been." But the novel was picked up by the Science Fiction Book Club in the fall of '62—fortunately for Phil, because it was the book-club edition that was widely read by science-fiction fans and thus made possible the turning-point event in Phil's career: winning the Hugo Award in September 1963 for the Best Science Fiction Novel of 1962.

It was an extraordinary turnaround. Phil's reputation in the science-fiction world had been at a low ebb. After three excellent novels at the beginning of his career (*Lottery, Jones,* and *Eye*), he had produced a series of minor novels (*Puppets, Futurity, Vulcan's*—actually reissues and rewrites of early works, but the readers had no way of knowing that) and an offbeat hybrid of mainstream novel and pulp sf *(Time out of Joint)* that most sf readers probably had never even seen. He wasn't writing short stories, it had been five years since his last significant novel was published—he was a has-been, a promising newcomer who hadn't panned out.

And then this magnificent book! Beautifully written, irresistible characters, a whole new approach to science-fiction storytelling—where did it come from?

I believe that the fact that Phil wasn't *trying* to achieve any specific career goal or to meet his own or anyone else's literary or editorial expectations probably had a lot to do with how well the book turned out. He had let go. He no longer had anything to lose. And so he could allow the book to write itself.

In my 1975 *Rolling Stone* article, Phil and I talk about what (we thought) happened next:

> In 1962, after *The Man in the High Castle* was published in hardcover and greeted with loud hurrahs, Phil wrote a novel called *Martian Time-Slip* which was just as good if not better. It's a novel about schizophrenia and contemporary life, autistic children, drugged housewives, power-crazed plumbers (on Mars), and the fragility of the systems of shared assumptions that hold human society together. The writing is humorous, painful, awesome in its effect on both mind and heart; the themes of the book anticipate R. D. Laing and many other gurus of the '60s and '70s; the quality of the prose, paragraph by paragraph, is exquisite. There are few modern novels to match it. But for the author, the book was, in his own words, "a crucial defeat."
>
> It was a defeat because of what happened after he finished writing it: "With *High Castle,* and *Martian Time-Slip,* I thought I had bridged the gap between the experimental mainstream novel and science fiction. Suddenly I'd found a way to do everything I wanted to do as a writer. I had in mind a whole series of books, a vision of a new kind of science fiction progressing from those two novels. Then *Time-Slip* was rejected by Putnam, and every other hardcover publisher we sent it to.

> "My vision collapsed. I was crushed. I had made a miscalculation somewhere, and I didn't know where. The evaluation I had made of myself, of the marketplace, went poof! I reverted to a more primitive concept of my writing. The books that might have followed *Time-Slip* were gone."
>
> *Martian Time-Slip* was eventually published by Ballantine as an original paperback in 1964. It has been out of print for seven years.

An interesting thing happened on my way to fleshing out the story of Phil's career for this book. I came across very convincing evidence that the above-quoted account is incorrect in some key details. *Martian Time-Slip* was never submitted to Putnam. There was another novel that Phil's agent, if not Phil, saw as the appropriate work to follow in the footsteps of *High Castle.* It was called *The First in Your Family.*

A major resource in my research into the chronology and events of Philip K. Dick's professional career has been the card file in which Phil's agent, the Scott Meredith Literary Agency, has kept track of every manuscript Phil ever sent them—its date of receipt, the magazines and book publishers it was submitted to, dates of sale, subsidiary-rights sales, and so forth.

These cards clearly indicate (and I have found ways of checking the accuracy of the cards, both by making sure they're internally consistent and by checking against PKD's dated correspondence, etc.) that the first recorded receipt by the agency of a manuscript from Phil following *High Castle* was a novel called *The First in Your Family* (finally published ten years later as *We Can Build You*), received October 4, 1962.

This novel was submitted the same day to Putnam, which had just published *High Castle.* Over the next four months, it was rejected by Putnam, Doubleday, Simon & Schuster, Ballantine, and Crown, all hardcover publishers except Ballantine. It didn't ultimately find a publisher until *Amazing Stories* magazine serialized it in 1969, and then Don

Wollheim, who had bought all of Phil's early novels at Ace, published it in 1972 through his new paperback imprint, DAW Books.

Later that same month, on October 31, 1962, Scott Meredith received from Phil another manuscript, this one entitled *Goodmember Arnie Kott of Mars.* Even given Phil's notorious difficulty with titles, it's hard to believe he intended this to be the book he would sell to Putnam to follow *High Castle*—it seems much more likely that he made this one sound pulpy in order that it not be confused with his new "serious" work, *The First in Your Family.* In any event, *Goodmember Arnie Kott* was indeed the book that Ballantine would later call *Martian Time-Slip,* and Scott Meredith's first move was not to submit it to a book publisher at all but to send it to a science-fiction magazine to have it serialized.

Goodmember sold for serialization in December 1962, and then Scott Meredith began marketing it to book publishers. The first three they tried—Ace, Berkley, and Pyramid—were paperback science-fiction publishers. They then tried Doubleday's hardcover sf line, and finally sold it to Ballantine in June of '63.

Clearly the agency never saw *Martian Time-Slip* as anything but a new sf adventure, and there's no reason to believe Phil thought any differently at the time. He may well have known how good it was (or, possibly, he may not have), but the evidence is that neither he nor his agent thought of it as having any chance outside of the hardcore science-fiction market.

The book Phil was really thinking of, when he talked about bridging the gap between his experimental mainstream novels and his science fiction, was *We Can Build You.* This is very much in the tradition of the mainstream novels Phil had been writing; and at the same time it has an authentic science-fiction element, in that it is about a mechanical man (charmingly, an android re-creation of Abraham Lincoln, who thinks he actually is Lincoln). It is more of a bridge, in a literal sense, than *High Castle;* the sad proof of that, ironically, is that by 1968 it was the only unsold science-fiction novel by PKD—because it was too close to mainstream.

But *We Can Build You* is also a flawed, or at least very idiosyncratic, novel, with much less of a resolved ending than *High Castle* (always the one weak spot of that fine book) and a rather rambling sense of auctorial purpose. It is a significant and worthwhile Philip K. Dick novel, perhaps the best expression of his theme of "the dark-haired girl," but it was a decidedly weak card to lead with in trying to capitalize (a year before the Hugo Award was announced, remember) on the hardcover publication of *High Castle.* This was not the book to unite science fiction and experimental mainstream in holy matrimony. Perhaps *Martian Time-Slip* could have been—although it seems quite unlikely, as it was far ahead of its time—but in any event it was never given the chance.

I have gone into this in detail because it was indeed a pivotal moment in Phil's career, but what actually transpired and the ways in which events in the marketplace influenced the future of Phil's writing are far more subtle, more elusive, than we might first want to believe. As in a Philip K. Dick novel, things are not what they seem, and they also may not be what we determine they are after we've looked a little closer. Did science-fiction ghettoization hold Phil back, or did it make his career and his novels possible? If *Martian Time-Slip,* or *We Can Build You,* had been published in hardcover as a breakthrough novel in 1963, would it have made a difference? Would Phil have written better books? I don't know. And neither did Phil know, any more than his characters know, when they're living one of his novels, whether the event that has just transpired—long-feared or long-hoped-for or totally unexpected—will in fact be their salvation or their doom or none of the above.

Turn the page and find out. Maybe.

CHAPTER SEVEN

THE BREAK-IN (CONTINUED)

CONVERSATION, *October 31, 1974*

WILLIAMS: Why did you start writing science fiction?

DICK: I don't know. I had ideas that could not be expressed any other way.

W: You tried to write mainstream fiction from the beginning, too.

D: Yeah.

W: You sent out short stories, too?

D: Yeah. Lots of 'em.

W: They didn't sell?

D: No. [weariness in his voice]

W: And the science fiction did?

D: Yes.

W: So in a sense, you didn't really end up with science fiction by choice.

D: No.

W: And obviously there was at least a period where you really wanted to break out of it.

D: Yeah. I tried again and again, desperately. Of course, now, you have to realize, as you do—I mean, it has to be taken into account—that in those days—we're talking about the early Fifties, the mid-Fifties—the state of science fiction was so crummy, the future was so bleak, the limitations were so enormous that there didn't seem to be any reason why an intelligent, educated adult with any literary ability would write science fiction. And our views, our conceptions were narrow. Our conceptions were mediocre. Our ideas of what we could be were mediocre, the field.

W: Who'd you hang out with in those days?

D: Poul Anderson, Jack Vance, Tony Boucher—um . . .

W: Now, Boucher was broader than science fiction. I mean, he had at least two careers, plus he was printed in a very respectable newspaper, as a critic.

D: That's true. He was a multifaceted and educated, brilliant and humane person. A fat lot of good it did him, too. To be all those things.

W: What do you mean?

D: Well, the first time I met Ted Sturgeon, the first thing he said to me was "What kind of universe is it, where Tony Boucher dies of bone cancer when he's fifty-six years old?" That's the first thing Ted Sturgeon said to me.

And I just stood there and stared at him. 'Cause I'd been thinking that ever since Tony died. Always the first thought in my mind, every day of my life, was *that* thought. And that Ted Sturgeon, when he met me, would say that—and later he asked me if I had known Tony! He didn't even know I knew him. Isn't that something?

In other words, it was the first thought in Ted Sturgeon's mind, "What kind of a universe are we living in?" That if ever there was a wonderful person, it was Tony Boucher. And if ever there was a senseless universe, it's the one we're in.

And I think that Tony's death *drove* us to writing better

fiction. Because we were faced with a much more incomprehensible world than we had realized. We'd sort of guessed until then, but after that we knew it.

It's as if Tony said, "Okay, I'm going to prove to you that science fiction is important. You're living in a weird universe. It isn't rational, it isn't meaningful." You know, the greatest incentive to write is that you can't figure out the universe. And you keep trying to do it by writing about it. You can coerce it into making sense by writing a book that makes sense, but what happens is, your books don't make any sense either.

W: So you start again.

D: So you start again, yeah, but, you say, "I'm gonna draw a model of the universe, and I'm gonna control the model, and I'm gonna follow the steps, one after another. When I get through, I'm gonna understand the model, 'cause I wrote it. And then I'm gonna look around, and I'll understand the universe, 'cause it's a model of it."

W: And about halfway through the book, the model starts to go transparent. Or fall apart. Or—

D: Go in funny directions that, um . . . [pause] The thing— You know, Tony Boucher's death affected everybody, because he had a perfectly organized life. That is to say, he was the way you ought to be. He had created an environment around him that was the way your environment ought to be. He was interested in everything that was worth being interested in. And all of a sudden he croaks from bone cancer. Misdiagnosed, because the doctor thought it was a broken rib. And taped it up. And when he removed the tape, he was dead. Because it had metastasized.

Now, how do you explain that? You're building a jigsaw puzzle, and you keep building it, and you have only one piece left, and you have one hole in the puzzle. You take the last piece and you start to put it in the last hole. And it doesn't fit. And since it doesn't fit, the whole puzzle is screwed up. You can never complete it. And while you're standing there looking at it, it just slowly falls into a million parts. That was the way we all felt.

W: When did he die?

D: Well, I dedicated *Ubik* to him, so he must have died pretty much just before. . . . He can't have died after *Ubik* was published. [Boucher died in 1968.]

He was an ardent Roman Catholic. Tony had, presumably, all the answers. And this was exhibited by, not fanaticism, but by the beautifulness of his life. Now, how can you have all the answers and have that happen?

He called me up before he died. He didn't know he had cancer. Nobody knew he had cancer. Including the doctor. We were talking on the phone one time. I said that I wasn't able to put in as many hours of work as I usually had in the past. He says, "That's true of me, too, Phil, I can only work half the day now, I feel so very tired." And we talked about maybe we had flu, or maybe it was the virus going around.

And with me it was depression, exhaustion, and nervous strain. With him it was fatal bone cancer. How do you like that? And he said, "What do you think it might be?" Isn't that a bummer? [angry]

W: So you wrote *A Maze of Death?*

D: Yes, that was—

W: Which is one of your most depressed books.

D: Yes.

W: In that book the characters are killed off, one by one, which doesn't happen in most of the books. They are separated.

D: And yet, there's an intervention by a divine figure that comes walking up to you when everything's all over for you. Right? Remember that part where he says, "What do you want to be?" and the guy says, "I want to be a cactus so the sun'll be shining on me all the time. That I could sleep, and feel it when I'm sleeping, even."

And you know, what happened was after *Ubik* I gave up, in a way, on the rational solutions—you know, the ones that make sense—and wrote a book that dealt—although you know I didn't mention Tony in it, I mentioned Jim—

That was another thing, is my friend Jim Pike croaked, at the same goddamn practically time! Before *A Maze of Death* came out, you know. Another ardent religious person. You got two, my two religious friends die within a year or so of each other.

They both had all the answers, and they were both into life completely, you know, completely into life, and everything. And I can't even say it screwed up my head by the time Jim died. I mean, by that time my head was so screwed up it didn't make any difference.

But it posed a problem for the rest of us, who were writing, you know. If we thought we were writing entertainment, or escapism, or something to earn a buck, we couldn't believe that after Tony died.

And I certainly couldn't believe that after Tony died, Jim died, and Nancy's mother committed suicide [Phil's fourth wife, Nancy, had a stepmother named Maren who was Bishop James Pike's mistress and is the basis of the character Kirsten in *The Transmigration of Timothy Archer*], Jim's son shot himself in the face with a shotgun while on an acid trip, and—uh, my cat ate rat poison [laughs crazily].

It was terrible, man, they were croaking like—they were falling around me like World War One, you know, just like in the end of *All Quiet on the Western Front,* you know, where the guy's finally down to him. And then Nancy went mad and—

W: You started hanging out strictly with young people, then.

D: That's true. Yes, you are quite right. After Nancy left, I just hung out with young kids. Although I'm not sure that was—oh, well, I mean, I'm sure that was deliberate. I mean to say that, that, uh [raises voice], why not? Everybody else was either dead or crazy! [chuckles] It was, you know, like the old had perished much before their time.

W: It's a way of searching for life, I would guess.

D: Yeah, that's true.

W: I mean, 'cause you could also go and hang out with your depressed friends who were the same age and drink a lot. I mean, I think that's really the choices.

D: Like at the end of *1984*, where they're all drinking synthetic gin, in the bar there . . . No, I went and plunged into a life of activity, you know, knife fights . . .

W: Stopped writing.

D: Yeah, stopped writing. When Nancy left, I finished *Flow My Tears* in rough . . . and then I never wrote again until '73 [two and a half years]. Well, who would? I mean, why? And what? And how? You know, I was paralyzed with—

W: You didn't even try to write, right? It wasn't a case of writer's block, you didn't try to write.

D: Exactly. I had enough professionalism in me to finish *Flow My Tears* in rough, and perfect it, go over it nine times and get it perfect, so it's just a typing job, turn over the manuscript to my attorney, for safekeeping, and then just give up. And as far as I knew, I would never write again. I never expected to write again. I expected to live off my residuals until I croaked. Whichever came first.

But, um—there really was no point in writing. As a matter of fact, when you conceive of how you write—one writes by going off into privacy, alone—one hour of solitude would have meant my demise, after Nancy left with my little girl. It was too risky. I had to be with people.

I flooded the house with people. Anybody was welcome. Because the sound of their voices, the sound of their activity, the din in the hall, anything, it kept me alive. I literally was unable to kill myself then, 'cause there was too much going on. It was a constant distraction.

And I got involved in their lives and their problems, see, thinking about them, worrying about them. I just overempathized with them in a hysterical way where their problems were mine. I no longer had an existence or an identity. Whatever happened to them happened to me. You know, it was a kind of vicarious life, through them.

And then when they all moved out finally, after November 17, '71, my house was hit, nobody would live with me, nobody would come in the door, practically. Out of fear, you know. They'd come in, see that, the ruins—and go back out. Then I was really alone.

W: Why don't you describe to me, for that opening that Tess suggested, you walked through the door and what you saw.

D: Well, the house looked fine from in front, outside, right, just any house, right?

W: You had a sense of foreboding?

D: None. Glad to be home.

W: You'd had a hassle with the car and you were just coming back to your—

D: Right. I was tired, it was late at night. . . . Early that morning I was sure the house was going to be hit that night. I had told Jodie that. . . . But by then I was so tired I'd forgotten all about it.

Opened the door—rubble all over the place! Smashed windows, smashed drawers, smashed—screens ripped off, asbestos from the fireproof file, which was saturated with water, all over the floor—

W: But you couldn't tell that it was asbestos right away.

D: Sure I could.

W: What did it look like?

D: It was white clay.

W: On the floor.

D: White clay on the floor. Yeah. I recognized it right away. I'd seen asbestos before. It couldn't be anything else. I mean, I could see the file. As I came in the door, to my left was the file, in the study. I looked—we had an open floor plan—I could look in, see the blown-open file and the tangled wreck that it was, and the pieces of asbestos—

W: It was literally blown up?

D: The top section, yeah. And I could see the color of the asbestos sheets carried out on the floor. I mean, I could see there was a match between them. I mean . . . a single glance: the blown file, the missing stereo, these very big speakers that I had—the enclosures weighed a hundred and fifty pounds apiece—they were gone; amplifier gone, changer gone; just glancing around—

W: What was your feeling?

D: You know what my feeling was? "Thank God!" You know why? Because, I had been saying, like Barbara had been saying before me, I had been saying to the police, and to my friends, and to myself, "I know I have enemies, I know they are going to hit this house, I know they are going to blow it apart."

And I had bought a gun, you know, for that reason, to protect myself. And my friends had said, "He's bought the gun to kill himself. He's crazy." This little chick come over and she says, "Your friends are saying you bought the gun 'cause you're crazy, and you're going to kill yourself." I says, "No, I know my house is going to be hit."

I had told everybody, as Barbara had; and when I looked around and saw, I says, "Thank God. My mind is more important than my possessions. I am not crazy, and Barbara wasn't crazy. We were right, I've got enemies, it's true."

I says, "At least my mind's intact." I'd rather have my m—I mean otherwise I would have been nuts, because she and I were in a state of absolute, abject terror. Standing there with a loaded gun, hour after hour in the dark, waiting for those people to burst in, and our friends saying, "They're nuts. They're crazy. Look at 'em!" And the police saying, "There's nothing, there's nothing going on here"—not "You're crazy" but "We found nothing," see? It was *relief* to see this. Because it proved that I wasn't nuts.

Now later I didn't feel that way, later, when I began to assess how much was missing, and began to assess the fact that if I had real enemies that would do this that my life was really in danger. When I started getting threatening phone calls, saying, "This is going to happen to you again, and it's going to be worse!"

W: You did get phone calls?

D: Yes.

W: What could you tell from the voices?

D: Oh, it was somebody I'd known who was crazy, who'd tried to get me.

W: You knew who was calling?

D: Yeah.

W: One theory of the break-in that you haven't mentioned in our talking, that you mentioned before, is the Minutemen.

D: Yeah. I was told by the, uh—one of the heroin rehab places there that I turned to, when I described it, they said immediately, "Oh, them? Oh, it's the Terra Linda Minutemen, they're the only ones who have the explosives that could do that."

W: This is a rehab center in San Rafael?

D: Yeah.

W: Terra Linda?

D: Terra Linda was a town there. And they said, "The Terra Linda Minutemen have that kind of explosives." And their M.O. was this: They blow up somebody who was left-wing, and they make it look like it was done by blacks. You see what I mean? They hang it on left-wingers. Even lefter-wingers.

W: This is to me a plausible—I mean, I have trouble with the federal-government theory, 'cause I just can't figure, you know, like you were making trouble on the local level, but apart from your books, which it's hard to connect, it's hard to tell, just to me—

D: It's tenuous, it's very tenuous, very speculative—

W: Yeah. But—well, there was this woman at the John Birch Society you were having arguments with—

D: Yes. Yeah. Oh, she was my friend. But she's married.

Her husband may have, you know, her husband may have been jealous.

W: They may have been talking, and he got the idea that this guy's a real . . . crank, a left-wing organizer. . . .

D: Oh, she considered me a Communist and so on, she called me a—

W: So even being your friend, she could—through that connection—I mean, there at least is some hint of some connection between—some consciousness of your activities among the right-wing community.

D: Absolutely. This was the first real clue, was when, at Centerpoint, they said, "Well, it's obvious. It's the Terra Linda Minutemen. Couldn't be anybody else. There's only two groups in Marin County that have military weapons, and only one that has explosives, and they try to make it look like it was left-wingers that did it—in other words, they score two things with one hit."

W: I mean, it is a good question: What the fuck did the black militants want with your canceled checks?

D: I can tell you right now, without going into the specifics, that you can almost surely eliminate the black militants.

W: Except that guy did have your gun.

D: He may have bought it.

W: And since he was never busted, he wouldn't have—he was never actually busted, as far as we know?

D: See, I can't find out. But there's certain—it's very complicated, but there are reasons that would indicate that it was not blacks, even though it was a black guy that was arrested with the gun. There were still reasons that would indicate it was not—very strongly indicate. The checks is one. There's really no reason why they would be getting the canceled checks, there's really no—that's a little more devious, you know, than the kind of thing they might be into as far as—but there's other reasons.

For one thing, I consulted with an American Nazi Party member and he told me flat out it was not black militants. He just said, "It was not black militants; I can tell you that." And I—

W: He came by; he looked around.

D: Yeah. Now, he would tend to pin it on blacks, being an American Nazi. That's one of the reasons why I kind of tend to go on what he said. I said, "Do you think it was blacks?" He said, "No, it was not blacks. I can guarantee you it was not blacks." But he didn't say anything else. He was very, you know, elliptical, but he said, "It was not the blacks." He says, "They've already extracted enough from you. It wasn't them."

W: What did he mean by that?

D: The high price they charged me for protecting that girl. About seven hundred and fifty dollars. He said, "They got all your money. They know it, you know it." He said, "You paid your debt to them." Now you see, being a Nazi, he would tend to be a racist and he'd tend to incriminate them if he could, but he said, "No, uh-uh, you must understand it was not the blacks."

W: They were protecting the girl against people she got involved with?

D: A junkie pusher she was trying to break away from. She wanted to be hospitalized. She asked me if I would take her to the hospital.

W: Did it work?

D: I got her in the hospital, yeah. [pause] She said she was quite ill. Umm, when I was trying to get her into the hospital, he showed up, and said he would kill her. That he knew her route from school—

W: The junkie.

D: Yeah. The pusher. And he would kill her. So I hired these guys to follow her and protect her. They did, and I got her into the hospital.

W: Good.

D: They were excellent. They were terrific. It was worth it. And the police came by and asked me their names, and I wouldn't give it to them. Well, for one thing, I didn't know their names. But they did their job beautifully.

W: What about San Rafael itself? I mean, a picture does emerge for me here. First of all, you were in a kind of a—

D: Yes, housing tract.

W: A housing development that dated back what, five, ten years?

D: Fifteen.

W: Fifteen years. Just kind of a side part of San Rafael?

D: Yeah, out in the boondocks. Out on the salt flats.

W: It's actually in Marin County jurisdiction rather than city jurisdiction?

D: Yes.

W: The police that came by were Marin County Police?

D: Marin County Sheriff's Office.

W: The mood of the city itself at this point—the Angela Davis trial was going on?

D: Correct. They were ferociously anti-black, anti-black-militant, anti—

W: After the shoot-out a year earlier?

D: Yes. Exactly. Cops were everywhere. When you went into the Hall of Justice or the Civic Center, you were searched by the police, you passed through a hoop. To see if you had any metal on you. The cops even examined literature you carried.

W: Nancy left you only a few weeks after that shoot-out?

D: Gee, see, I didn't know that—

W: I'm trying to remember the dates—

D: It's possible.

W: No awareness at that time.

D: No. Nancy was a member of the Angela Davis Defense Committee, though, and quite active in it, and was fingerprinted by the FBI. Now, about the Minutemen . . .

W: Right.

D: That was the first and most obvious thought. And you'd think that I would just have stuck with that. It seemed perfectly obvious. But um . . . if they did it, they had the collusion of the authorities, in the sense that the authorities stood back and let them do it.

And that's possible. But then there's Jodie saying that inspector wanted to set me up and have me thrown in the bucket, on a serious rap. There was the guy hiding drugs. Those are not Minutemen, those are not Birchers. They're something else.

And, uh—there are other things that point to something else. Although this is what I first thought, that it was a private paramilitary group that hit the house. But I do not think it was.

Although I don't know who did it. Almost every theory will work as well as every other theory on this, and all the possibilities we've talked about are equally plausible.

I'll tell you another possibility: a series of hits that night. By drug enforcement. By criminals, afterward. Or vice versa.

W: Were you away for a long time?

D: Yes. A series of waves, you know . . .

W: Suppose you'd come back while it was going on?

D: Oh . . . my American Nazi friend said I would have been killed. There's no doubt about that. But the tip on the phone said it'd been done by the police. And blacks. Together. Makes no sense.

[An article in the April 1980 issue of *Penthouse* magazine describes some of the activities of one of a number of FBI-hired operatives whose job was to infiltrate radical groups and promote or execute disruptive activities. The prime target of this operation, particularly circa 1969–71, was radical black groups; the black operative (code-named Othello) who is interviewed in the *Penthouse* article "provided detailed layouts of the offices of Hollywood personalities who were known to have given money to black organizations . . . all of which ‹offices› were later burglarized." He claims to have carried out many other activities, some of them far more violent and many of them quite irrational, even given the program's aims. Reports like this, and other information that has started coming out about FBI "Cointelpro" activities, make some of Phil's more farfetched theories about the break-in sound quite believable.]

All these things are equally possible. In an area so volatile, with so many militant groups, so many weapons . . . And after all, a lot of people thought it was me. Nancy told me in 1972, in November of '72, during the divorce, "You know, they say you did it yourself." So that was a theory, that I had done it. That was one possibility.

W: How would you have done it? I mean—

D: Well, I couldn't have done it. But some people thought I did.

W: What was their theory? I mean, that you did it—

D: To cover my tracks. To cover my real activities. Which were so sinister that it was worth doing that, to cover it up.

W: Or to prove that your paranoias had been true all along?

D: Uh-huh. I suppose so.

W: There's somebody I'd like to talk to, if you have any idea where she is: Barbara [not her real name].

D: No way to find her; she disappeared completely. I tried to find her. . . .

W: Who was she? You don't—except by name, you don't talk about her much in *The Dark-Haired Girl*, or—

D: Well, she was just a crummy street broad that used to hustle nickels and dimes and turn tricks, I guess, and shoot up heroin, and drop stuff, and looked like any other little crummy street broad about eighteen years old that had nothing on the ball, and she came by with her boyfriend, to take refuge there— I knew him. And let 'em stay. They didn't have anyplace to go, she was pregnant.

And after a while I realized that she was an incredibly gifted, brilliant person. And I hung on to her as long as I could. Just trying to watch that spark of beauty and intelligence in her head grow.

But she slipped away. 'Cause she wasn't interested in that. It was tragic, that her motivations were at variance with her talents. But she was—except for Tess; she and Tess are the two most brilliant people I've ever known. And Tess is motivated along with her brilliance; but Barbara was motivated to hustle her ass for nickels and dimes.

And yet—she could take, Paul, she could take this book of poetry here, six centuries of great poetry, and look through, and find one really high-class sonnet out of them. I found her once copying out an early sonnet. A pre-Shakespearean sonnet, I think Sir Philip Sidney. She was copying out a sonnet by Sir Philip Sidney.

So I says, "How come you're copying that out?" And she says, "Well, this expresses my feelings." Sir Philip Sidney. She's copying it out laboriously. And I read it over, and I looked through the whole book, and I couldn't find one that was much better. After she had looked through the whole book, she decided that *that* was what expressed her sentiments the most. She could do that.

I watched her pick out *Finnegans Wake* and Milton's *Paradise Lost*—can you dig it?—and she was reading, looking at *Finnegans Wake* one day, she says, "Hey! The only way to read this is aloud! You gotta read this aloud." And so she did. And she'd sit down these raunchy, motherfucking dudes, these punks, and she'd read aloud to them from *Paradise Lost.*

W: Who were the guys? We still haven't talked about them.

D: Just bums that she knew.

W: Hippies?

D: Oh, no, man, uh, guys that rotated tires in gas stations.

W: They'd drop by the house, too, listen to the Grateful Dead. . . ?

D: Yeah.

W: Smoke grass . . . I mean, I guess they just considered it a place—

D: Place to hang out?

W: Yeah.

D: I guess so.

W: I mean, for a lot of the kids—

D: Well, weren't that many kids. With my speaker systems—these Fender Bassman bottoms are really for amplifiers for electric guitars; people used to come with electric guitars—rock-band types, amateurs, would come in and use it that way. A lot of the people I met in connection with that kind of thing, with guitars. That's how I got interested in rock. I didn't know anything about rock until then. I finally really got into it.

They played cards. . . .

CONVERSATION, *later the same day (Phil is already talking when the tape starts.)*

D: . . . first time. Second time I met the Special Forces guy. The first time I was talking to an attorney—

W: In the hospital in Marin?

D: Yeah. No, no, in the hospital down here, in Fullerton, this year when I was in for high blood pressure. And I described the hit on the house.

And he says, "You were a friend of Jim Pike's, weren't you?" I think we discussed it, I don't think he knew that from just plucking it out of the air. I said, "Yeah." He says, "Well, I know quite a bit is popularly known about Jim Pike, the religious stuff, but also the occult stuff that Jim got into, the business about being contacted by his son from the other side.

"Now, is there any possibility your house was hit by some kind of religious fanatic group? I would bet that it wasn't political, or anything like that. It wasn't federal, and it wasn't any kind of right-wing paramilitary thing." He says, "I'll betcha that it was religious." He says, "I'll betcha it's because you were known to have been a friend of Jim's. And Jim was into some heavy shit at the end of his life, some really heavy shit.

"Now," he says, "what was the last book that you'd had come out?" I says, *"A Maze of Death."* He says—just a second now, I'll read you this [rummages around, comes up with a copy of the book]. He says, "Tell me about your book previous to the hit on the house." [Phil reads from the book] *"A Maze of Death."* And it says in the foreword, "The theology in this novel," and so forth, uh, ". . . based on the arbitrary postulate that God exists. I should say, too, that the late Bishop James A. Pike, in discussions with me, brought forth a wealth of theological material for my inspection, none of which I was previously acquainted with."

Now, the lawyer didn't know about this paragraph. I went home and looked it up after I got out of the hospital. Which is interesting, because his speculation was, "They may have thought you had documents, notes, pertaining to things that Jim was into, in terms of religious heresy, and the occult, and that's what they were looking for."

And here's this thing, "The late Bishop Pike, in discussion with me, brought forth a wealth of theological material for my inspection, none of which I was previously acquainted with." And this whole novel is a religious novel. Okay. Somebody reading this would think, I'll betcha he's got some, either of Jim's notes—and I'm mentioned in the foreword to Jim's book, *The Other Side,* which is his book about being contacted by his son—see? I'm mentioned there, Jim is mentioned here. Somebody reading this would think, This heretical and occult stuff Jim was into, Phil Dick has got notes on. And they hit the house for those notes. Now that's what the lawyer said. And I looked at the date on this book. July '71 is when the paperback came out. Four months before the hit on the house.

W: What did it say about you in the intro to Jim Pike's book?

D: It just thanked me and Nancy for helping in doing research, I think. That's what we did, we did research on these occult phenomena for him.

W: Great. Great. The religious-fanatic theory.

Okay, now I'm trying to make a list here. These are the possibilities that we've discussed; see if I left any out. Uh . . . black militant terrorists.

D: Mm-hm. Tess, you listen and see if this list is complete, okay?

T: I'm listening.

W: Minutemen or some kind of right-wing commando group.

D: Yeah.

W: Local police, or narcs [narcotics agents].

D: Yeah.

W: Federal Watergate-type agents.

D: Yeah.

W: Or narcs or whatever. Religious fanatics. Uh, drug-crazed rip-off artists—

D: Yeah.

W: —from the youth community. Uh, the police theory that you did it yourself.

D: Mm-hm.

W: How many others have we got?

D: Military agents, that's different from all the others.

W: Military agents, à la Special Forces?

D: Yes. The air force or army, that kind of thing.

W: Because of the—

D: I was near Hamilton Air Force Base, for one thing.

W: That they would have done it because of the thing in *Penultimate Truth,* or that kind of . . . [Phil had speculated that a minor plot idea in that particular novel, involving nerve gas, might have been a description of an actual secret weapon, and therefore a motive for an investigative hit. And in a 1978 interview with Joe Vitale, still talking about the break-in, Phil referred to that novel saying, "In the early

Sixties I did write a novel about a phony war between the United States and Russia that's carried out with the sole purpose of keeping the citizens of those countries underground, while the leaders live in palatial splendor aboveground. Now maybe certain people thought this was too close to the truth and that I had some kind of information. Maybe that's why they wanted to get my files. I don't know."]

D: Possibly, yeah. I mean, this is just a possibility, air force.

W: Yeah, I had them sort of put in my mind with the federal.

D: Yeah. But it should be separate.

W: Uh-huh. What would the motive be for a Watergate-type break-in?

D: All right, I'll tell you something. Something real; this is not speculation. On January 1, that's after this, the subsequent January 1, an attempt was made on the arsenal at the Hamilton Air Force Base, to steal all the weapons. The only reason it failed was the arsenal had been moved. They got what was left, which was CO_2 guns. Now, obviously that would be terrorist groups, or, this is to sell it to terrorist groups, this would be automatic weapons, illegal automatic weapons.

And I had heard, from people in Marin County, that the right-wing and the left-wing people in Marin County—that is, black militants and Minutemen—were training in the hills, with semiautomatic weapons. I myself heard, in the boondocks, when I lived up in west Marin [this would have been 1964 or earlier], I heard machine-gun fire, or semiautomatic fire, on remote ranches. I heard it with my own ears. A deputy sheriff told me those guys were using weapons of that kind.

But anyway, the attempt was made on this air-force arsenal, January 1, right after the hit.

W: But why would there have been an attempt on your house?

D: Okay. Several of the people I knew—this is for off the record. Don't for God's sake put this in. You can tape it if you want, but don't put it in writing.

Several of the people I knew were, um, they were not air-force personnel, but they had access to Hamilton. They were minors whose parents were air-force personnel, a number of them. See? They came and went from Hamilton. And they were into illegal activities. And they were close friends of mine. And the same people—

Well, okay, I'll tell you. Now this is just really off the record, gotta be for sure off the record. I think you'd better turn the tape recorder off. [I turned it off.]

A little later in the evening, not immediately after the "off the record" discussion, I turned on the tape to pick up a conversation in progress, our last taped discussion of the break-in.

D: . . . virulent racist blacks. Not my friends, not my friends the blacks, but really bad criminal blacks.

W: You were hit by black terrorists who wanted to drive you out?

D: Yeah, but that's only part of it, a little bit of it. That's hardly any of it. Want to know how I figured it out?

I just suddenly realized, the guy, the air-force guy [some kind of air-force investigator who came to see him, apparently], showed me a picture of the same guy as the local police did, and they said he was in Q [San Quentin Prison], a black guy from the house behind me. I just suddenly visualized it. They were very interested in identifying that one guy.

In other words, they both showed me pictures—

W: They knew who he was—

D: But that was the only picture that they both showed me, you see. The same picture showed up twice. They were both very interested. And they were very upset when I didn't recognize him.

Now. Here's what it was. There was a black terrorist group forming.

W: He wasn't the guy that was found with the gun?

D: No.

W: He wasn't somebody that you knew, this one guy?

D: Correct. That's the problem. This particular guy, who lived in the house behind me, who had lived and was no longer there, but had access to it, because it was his family—he was the oldest brother, you see; he could come back any time—was really insane. He was the one that drove the whites out before me, you see, at knifepoint, threatened to kill them if they didn't move out. Okay. There was a black terrorist group that I had no contact with, and I knew nothing about it.

Now, here's what happened. The authorities had been watching all this, the black terrorist group, this guy specifically, they had his picture, and they were very interested in him. They knew these guys were into automatic, semi-automatic weapons and stuff like that, that this was like the SLA, like a military uprising.

But the authorities didn't want to tip their hand. They didn't want to reveal to the terrorists, to the blacks, that they knew *anything* about their existence. That's why . . . I suddenly realized. You see, the blacks hit me; and then there was a hands-off policy on investigating that hit. Because if they had followed up the hit on my place, they would be forced—

W: They would tip their hand too soon.

D: Too soon. You see, in dope circles, you know, the policy is to not bust the little people but to follow it up as far as possible—

W: The blacks wanted to drive you out. I mean, that was—

D: They had a very limited objective, just to force a white family out. But you see, the police, if they'd come in and busted them—

W: Were there many white families left in the neighborhood?

D: Very few. If the police had busted 'em, then they would have upset their plans of watching and surveilling and going higher up into this, see, to see where the source of it was. They would have busted a couple of penny-ante black hoods for a small matter.

W: How long had you been in that house, by the way?

D: About two and a half, three years. I just flashed on it, man. See the blacks had a very limited objective. The police were in a terrible position. They actually knew who had hit my house. . . .

The tape ends at this point. There were other theories, too, that never got on tape. And I have no doubt that if I'd stuck around a few more evenings, there would have been some new ones.

In the *Rolling Stone* article, I organized the theories by number: fourth theory of the break-in, fifth theory, etc. My editor made me cut out a few theories when the piece got too long. The fifth theory is apparently the one that we discussed with the tape turned off—probably I got Phil's permission to talk about it, since I know he saw and enthusiastically approved the manuscript as soon as I finished it. Here's what I wrote:

> This theory has strange parallels with Phil's forthcoming novel *A Scanner Darkly*. *Scanner* is a portrait of the drug subculture, probably the best that's ever been written, full of black humor and painfully real human beings. These people are burning their brains out, without realizing it, on a drug Phil invented—in the opening chapter there's a guy taking fifty showers a day trying to wash the imaginary bugs off his body.
>
> The novel is about a narc who is assigned to cover himself. In this slightly future situation, narcs wear electronic scanners when they give their reports, so their superiors, who

could be Mob infiltrators, don't know their real identities. Thus a person can easily be assigned to report on his own activities. What happens to our narc is he's taking the drug (nicknamed "death") so as to blend in with everyone else, and it's rotting his brain. Eventually he no longer knows that the person he's reporting on is himself—and he gets more and more fascinated, more and more suspicious. . . .

As for the theory: Phil heard, back at the time that our story takes place, that a military disorientation drug had been stolen from the army and was being used in street dope under the name "mello jello." The drug incapacitated people without their realizing it, it bonded in their cellular tissue (says Phil); and the army wanted, not to make a bust, but to get their compound back.

And there was a guy hanging around Phil's house, a truly sinister character, who told Phil he secretly represented a health organization trying to track down the source and spread of a spirochete brought back from Vietnam that induced rapid tertiary syphilis. The symptoms he described resembled the cumulative effects of "mello jello."

Phil had plenty of reason, he says, to wonder about this guy—for example, when he was very stoned he asked Phil, "Would you believe I ever looked like this?" and showed him a picture. The picture was on an Air Force ID card. And when he and Phil were stopped by the police one day, the cops took one look at the guy and said, "You're Army, aren't you?" "Yes," he said, and the cops split.

Theory: The guy was a military intelligence agent, looking for users of "mello jello." The house was hit by a branch of the military, trying to get information that would help them get their drugs back.

. . . Looking over my notes, I realize I could go on and on. But the main thing is not "What could have happened?" The main thing is "What did happen?" Isn't it? I'm not too sure anymore.

Saturday morning, three days after my arrival in Fullerton (during which time Phil and I left the house only once, to visit, at my request, the university library that houses the

Philip K. Dick collection), I packed my tapes and my papers, thanked Tessa for her cooking, and said goodbye to Phil and Christopher.

I was on my way to Marin County, to the city of San Rafael, to search for a reality perspective of my own.

CHAPTER EIGHT

AMPHETAMINES AND AMNESIA

CONVERSATION, *October 30, 1974*

WILLIAMS: I wanted to ask you, you mentioned to me way back in like 1970, I guess before you finished *Flow My Tears,* that you felt that it really affected your ability to write that you couldn't—that your doctor made you give up amphetamines and everything, altogether. [pause]

DICK: Um. What affected me was the depression that set in, which was there before, which I thought . . .

W: Which you were avoiding . . .

D: Yeah, in other words, I took the amphetamines because I was depressed. I was completely wrong as to why I took them. I thought I took 'em to write. I took 'em to overthrow a depression. Once the depression was overthrown, then I could write or anything else, you know.

And then I stopped taking all medication . . . ah, shit, when was that? It's been years now. Well, before I went to Canada. So let's say around the end of '71. And I continued depressed for quite a while.

W: And you didn't write.

D: And I didn't write. Went to Canada in early '72. Well, I was in no position to write there. Didn't really even have a typewriter. The depression got worse; I tried to kill myself. Went in the heroin rehab place 'cause they would watch me all the time.

That was a thing we set up with the crisis center, the crisis center suggested it. They said, "Well, you're going to have to be watched night and day or you'll kill yourself, so you tell 'em, you know, that you're a junkie or something like that, and they'll watch you."

They used to say to me [at the rehab place], "If you leave here, you'll stick that spike up your ass." And they used to say, "Don't go back on junk, Phil." And I'd say, "I never will, I'll never go back, I'll never shoot junk."

But the depression continued, and then '73—was that when I typed up *Flow My Tears,* Tess, the final on that?

TESSA: Uh, yeah.

D: Yeah. After my divorce from Nancy, in October of '72, that's two years ago—as soon as we got divorced, I was able to write again. I just realized. You know, I hadn't thought of that. But dating it, I wrote a story, I wrote "A Little Something for Us Tempunauts." Then I typed up *Flow My Tears,* I revised it again and typed it up. And then I wrote *Scanner Darkly.* You see what I mean? As soon as I got divorced and I was free to marry Tess and everything, I began to write again.

I wrote furiously, man. Oh, sheez. And I wasn't taking anything. And I was able to turn out as—well, like this screenplay, the *Ubik* screenplay, in three weeks. You see, that's as much as a person could write, and I wasn't taking anything.

T: Well, when he wrote "A Little Something for Us Tempunauts," when he finished it, he got up from the typing chair and passed out, right on the floor.

D: [defensively] Well, I had pneumonia, though, see. You

know, that is funny, I was able to work myself over long periods of time very hard, as if, if you saw me I'd look like I was taking amphetamines or something, 'cause I drove myself and drove myself. . . .

W: Adrenaline.

D: Yeah. But you see, I thought, I really thought that if I didn't take 'em I couldn't write. And in a way that was true. But the reason I couldn't write was the depression. And it required a lifting of the depression, due to a change in my life circumstances, a brightening of my hopes, you see.

W: When did you start taking them?

D: Well . . . in the Fifties.

W: So really early on in your writing career.

D: Yeah. Um, by the time I wrote *Eye in the Sky.* And I attributed my speed of writing, my rapidity, and my high productivity, and my pushing myself, to the amphetamines. And then I find now that I do exactly the same.

W: Without.

D: You know, what's really wild, I even crash the same way. I have to pay the same dues. I finish, like the screenplay, and I felt just as rotten as if I'd been taking amphetamines and was coming off them. In other words, I've got everything the same, everything I attributed, good and bad, either one, I got anyway. And it's been so many years now, see, '72, '73, and we're into the end of '74. I even got hair-trigger anger. It's identical.

And this confirms a diagnosis I got once, that they discovered something odd about me, and that was that when I took amphetamines my liver detoxified them and excreted them through the urine, or something like that. Anyway they never reached my brain, they said; the blood tests show they never entered my bloodstream, or anyway never reached the neural tissue. And they said that they thought that I took them for psychological reasons.

W: In other words, it's like you were taking placebos the whole time, in a sense.

D: Yeah, and when I consider what they cost me, it's sort of irksome.

W: [laughing] Well, if they'd been cheaper, they wouldn't have worked.

D: If they'd cost more, they would have worked better.

They said they were baffled that I would take something that their tests showed never reached my brain. They actually took blood tests of me as I took them, and they said it goes into the body and reaches the liver and is detoxified there—transformed, and eliminated as toxins. They said it's really odd to see somebody do that.

I think part of it was that I was living in a drug subculture, and that we don't realize the extent to which we're influenced by our environment, that everybody else was taking some form of drugs, and I wouldn't have known how to have behaved if I didn't have something to take. [It didn't occur to me at the time to ask Phil why he started taking speed ten years before he got involved with any "drug subculture."]

W: This wouldn't apply to tranks and Valium and that sort of thing?

D: No, it was specifically about the amphetamines. My liver identified them as toxins, and simply excreted them. And the doctors said that also explained why it didn't matter how many I took. And I said, "Well, that explains why I like to take some in order to go to sleep at night."

Two days later, on November 1, 1974, we discussed this some more.

W: So almost everything until now—which means until *Scanner* and the revision of *Flow My Tears*—was written on speed to some extent. Is that an exaggeration?

D: Mmm . . . No, that's not an exaggeration. That's correct.

Scanner is the first complete novel I had written [after giving up drugs], started from scratch, and I found myself doing exactly what I'd done when I'd taken amphetamines—that is, I would work incredibly long hours, eat very little, sleep almost—

W: How long?

D: All the goddamn time, from the time I got up in the morning until just drop at night, you know—we're talking about more than the number of hours per day, nothing but write. And each day get up and write, and write and write and write until I went to bed, and then get up the next day and write and write and write.

T: He used to, like, go to bed at two-thirty; and at three he'd say, "I've got to write this down!" and get up and work another hour. And get up at like seven in the morning and just work all day.

D: If you'd watched me, you would have thought I was taking speed, I guess. And then, when I got toward the end, I was all dingy and screwed up, and then, you know, I crashed. And it was all like withdrawal, and it's been years since I've taken amphetamines, actually a matter of years.

It's obvious that my system generates the conditions necessary, that—what we're talking about here, really, which I didn't realize, is a work habit. It's a way of producing a novel. That I don't make notes; and if I don't make notes, if I do a little each day, I'm gonna forget the continuity, I'm not gonna be able to pick it up again. And that the only way I can really do it is just to continue to do it until it's done.

Ideally I'd like to sit down and start writing and write all the way through to the end. Without any breaks whatsoever.

W: Most of your novels are done in a relatively short period of time?

D: Absolutely. Yeah. From two weeks on.

W: Up to a couple of months? I mean, the actual writing.

D: Yeah, exactly.

W: How long was *Scanner,* for example?

D: How long did I work on *Scanner,* dear?

T: Uh . . . two months?

D: Okay, two months.

W: That's extraordinary.

D: Yeah, And in the middle I took off to go autograph books for two or three days. But I never thought of anything else. It [not taking speed] had no effect on my work habits. None whatsoever. My work habits remained the same. I mean, I had no other conception of how to write a novel than to just sit down and begin to write, and write till I'm finished. Just push through, you know, it's a—like one great heroic push, tour de force, it's a continual tour de force.

W: When I saw you at the beginning of 1970, you were saying that—which probably is a feeling any writer gets a lot of times—that you couldn't write, and that it was partly because you'd had to stop taking speed. That your doctor had said that your liver—

D: Yeah, right. See, that is really fascinating to me, you know, that I believed there was a direct connection between the amphetamines and the writing. And what I realize now is it was like a primitive ritual which I went through, that I attributed to them a potency . . . like a person who's gotta have a rabbit's foot; without that, he has no good luck, you know. Or like your teddy bear. If you don't have your teddy bear with you, it's all over. . . . And if I didn't have them, I couldn't write. I completely psyched myself into that. That they were essential to me. I'd built up a whole mystique about it.

Then in '71, at the Hoover Pavilion Hospital, Stanford Hospital, I was diagnosed, given a complete physical, and they told me that the amphetamines never even reached my brain. They were detoxified by my liver, and never—

W: This was after you were in the—

D: I was thrown in by my girlfriend, who thought I was a drug addict. I didn't mention that to you?

W: No.

D: It's a funny—it's another funny story like my suicide stories.

I was living down there in, uh, Palo Alto with this completely burned-out broad who had been shooting speed at one time and dropping it and—

W: Another period where you just left the house for a while . . .

D: Yeah. I lived down there. I was going to move in with her and marry her and everything like that. And she had been—had shot speed and had dropped acid, and been in the mental hospital. She was really burned out, crazy. And we were living together and we were kind of quarreling.

And one day she came home with her psychiatrist, and they told me they were throwing me into the mental hospital because I was a drug addict and I should be detoxified. And I says, "No, you're not, I'm gonna go back to San Rafael." And she says, "No, you're not, because it's my car. Your car's still up in San Rafael. It's sixty miles, you've got—no way you can get back. You haven't got any money, so what the hell are you gonna do?"

So I says, "You know—" And she says, "You're not gonna stay here. I'll just throw you out the door, otherwise." And he said [low voice], "You'd better do it, Phil, you're a drug addict."

So I went into Hoover Pavilion, for detoxification, which is about a month thing, and the fee is about two thousand dollars.

W: Jesus.

D: They really had me by the balls. If I was ever had by the balls, that was it.

Now, he was protecting his patient; she was his patient, and she couldn't stand the clash of us living together. And this was an awful easy solution for her, but an awful rough solution for me.

So they threw me in for detoxification, and presented me with no alternative whatsoever, except to walk sixty miles or hitchhike. And they explained to me that I was so wired and spaced and strung out that I obviously would never make it back to San Rafael. Well, when a psychiatrist tells you these things, it sounds real, you know, it's like police. So I says, "Yeah." But I resented it, though; I wasn't happy.

So I went in there. It was a nice hospital. And the next morning I met this really pretty girl there. And I started telling her I was a great writer, which is—which I guess, well, I'm not sure if that's an indication of being wired, strung out and spaced and all that, but I had Elly bring in one of my novels, *Three Stigmata,* and I spent the whole day showing the girl this book and talking to her.

Since I really didn't know what to do . . . I'd never been detoxified before, I'd never been in a mental hospital, I just . . . She was an awfully pretty girl, and I just sat and rapped with her and showed her the book and went on and on and on. Which is what I normally do anyway. Except I was inside looking out, rather than outside looking in.

And, uh, they gave me some Librium, you know, that was nice. And the next morning the psychiatrist said, "You're leaving." And I said, "But I'm supposed to be in here for like two weeks or three weeks or a month or something."

He says, "No." Well, they gave me these physical exams, too. He says, "You've been diagnosed. You've been diagnosed all this time that you've been sitting here talking to this girl." He says, "You're not a drug addict."

I read the written thing—it was read to me, a report all four of them signed. That their physical tests, and their observation, showed that I was not an addict; that if I needed to be detoxified, I wouldn't have been sitting here the next day rapping to this chick—I mean, this is their expertise at work, this is what they do. First there's diagnosis, before anything else—before they detoxify somebody for two thousand a month, they find out if they've got somebody in there that needs that done to them.

W: Thank God.

D: Thank God, right. It still cost me something like three hundred and fifty bucks.

But they said, "Go home, you're fine, there's nothing wrong with you. I mean, there's no reason to keep you here." They had people there who were not addicts, too—it was a general funny farm—and they said, "Go home."

The consensus of the physical and psychological tests was that the amphetamines were not affecting me physically, that I took them for other reasons but they didn't know why I took them. That they were not actually reaching neural tissue, that they were excreted through the detoxifying process of the liver. Which they said would not be true if I ever were to shoot it, because then I would bypass the liver. One psychiatrist was quite angry that I was there at all, angry at the girl—he couldn't be angry at the girl's psychiatrist, he couldn't do that, that's against—

W: Professional ethics.

D: Right. But he thought I'd been railroaded in there, and he got me right out.

She wouldn't let me back in the apartment, so I went back to San Rafael. And I was fine, you know. And they recommended to my psychiatrist up there that I be rediagnosed, that I had been misdiagnosed by him and by my previous psychiatrist, that I was a completely different personality type than had been realized.

And then, talking to the doctor later, I found out that their diagnosis there at the Hoover Pavilion is extremely good and extremely precise and accurate, and to depend on that over anybody else's, and always to hang on to that.

And they said that I would probably continue to take amphetamines for whatever unknown reason it was that I took them, and when the time came when it no longer served a purpose, I would drop them just like that. And so I did, just a few months later.

W: What was your concern about your liver, when I'd met you before that?

D: Well, I had had pancreatitis. And because of that there

had been some liver damage, or liver disturbance, a dysfunction of the liver. And that was always a worry, you see. Because if I were ever to get hepatitis, I would die, since with the pancreatitis having occurred I could never secrete bile and it would be totally fatal and no way out.

W: Any kind of hepatitis?

D: Well, infectious hepatitis. Well, maybe any kind, for all I know.

W: So that was also why, at that point, you didn't want to take any more liver-toxic drugs?

D: I guess so. I forgot about that. Because after, when I was in Hoover Pavilion and they told me that my liver was detoxifying so effectively, I guess I forgot that my liver ever had an amylase disturbance, you see. I mean, I was very proud of my liver, and I frequently referred to it as the finest part of me, my brain coming in a bad second.

But I felt really good when I heard their concurrent diagnosis, that I wasn't an addict, that I took it for some kind of strange reason—which I now think was protective coloration. You see what I mean? By living in that culture, and taking it, I blended, and if I had acted as crazy as I was . . .

W: Were people doing stuff like—I mean other people must have been shooting, but—

D: Well, I never saw anybody in my life shoot dope.

W: Never?

D: Never.

W: So the kids you were dealing with, in that sense, there weren't that many that were really hardcore A-heads or junkies?

D: There was one girl that was shooting, uh, crank. But I never saw her do it. And I didn't know she was doing it until after a while. And I understand some of them were junkies, but they never told me, and I never saw them shoot. And I've never seen smack, and I've never seen anybody shoot anything.

W: They were taking meth and stuff like that, or—

D: Mostly just grass, grass and hash, a lot of hash pipes around.

W: That won't burn out your brains.

D: I know. That's why I'm pretty sure that a lot of them were shooting smack, because they were burning out. . . .

W: Or speed. I mean, you can easily get burned out on speed, and sometimes it's more attractive to young people.

D: Yeah, well, I think that there were combinations. They would take smack and then they would nod out, and then they would shoot crank and stay awake, and finally they didn't know the difference anymore.

This one girl did finally tell me that she had started out shooting smack and then she started shooting speed. I met her at a rehab place. But that's the first insight I got. In Canada I learned a lot more. But I also learned that junkies don't tend to tell you they're junkies. Because they're gonna rip you off, and if they tell you they're junkies, then you're—

W: But you can tell.

D: I couldn't. I didn't know. It was only later, in Canada, at X-Kalay, I described some of the people's behavior, and they said, "Those were for sure junkies, no doubt about it." The syndrome, all the various points that would show up, all of them showed up. The mysterious occurrences of different kinds. . . .

I was very naïve. But let me say one thing that I think is really very important, just between you and me, and Sasha here [the cat]. Is that after Nancy left, I was so depressed, and so crazy from grief, and loneliness, that I really was very unaware of what was going on in my environment. I didn't understand my environment. I wouldn't have understood this situation here, you and me sitting here talking, Tess there and the baby—you know what I mean? I just simply was out of it. From the shock.

W: Like characters in your books, gravitating towards any situation that had people in it, as opposed to being alone.

D: Exactly, exactly. But the main thing was that the shock of Nancy leaving—it was sudden, when she left. I didn't understand, and I didn't understand anything after that. I really didn't understand my environment anymore; it became incoherent to me, and I became incoherent to it.

W: Even though all the pressures and everything were there before she left?

D: Yeah. I was doing pretty good, in a way, for a while. She was mentally ill for a number of years. . . . That's another thing, I began to suffer serious amnesia—

W: Amnesia?

D: Yeah, very serious amnesia. It's only during the therapy I had in the last year here in Orange County that the therapist was able to make clear to me that I suffered radical amnesia.

I had blocked out perhaps as much as a year or two years, in all, of things that happened to me before Nancy left—terrible things; she was in the hospital more than once, and I had repressed all of these events. And it was because in '64, my automobile accident, I had amnesia after that; and when these terrible things began to happen, in 1968 and '9, amnesia was a mechanism my mind had learned, see. So there's lots of parts that I just blocked out, that only recently, only within the last few months, have I begun to remember, whole basic episodes blocked out.

I started to have amnesia again down here, after I married Tess—didn't I, dear? Just before the baby was born, I began to show periods of amnesia. That's what got me into therapy here in Orange County, you see.

W: Clinic kind of therapy, or—

D: Well, clinic, yeah, but I had my own therapist. And amnesia was one of the pronounced symptoms of my condition. And they found it went back to the automobile accident in '64; my mind had learned to do it when I was in the state of pressure and shock. And then I discovered I'd been doing it in 1968 and 1970 and after that.

So apparently, during the last year or so when I was with Nancy, I had repressed a lot of that; and subsequent to Nancy's leaving, there were periods of amnesia, too. Some of which I'm sure I still don't remember. May never remember.

Serious amnesia. The real thing. When things got really bad, miserable and wretched, you know, or I got really frightened, I began to blank out, retrospectively.

It'd be like, an example would be, suppose tomorrow you fly away from here, and if this was all a traumatic experience, or if there was a lot of anxiety in it for me, would be that next week I would say to Tess, "Gee, I wonder when Paul Williams is gonna come and interview me," see? And she'd say, "He just did, last week!" And I'd say, "I don't remember it at all."

It'd be that basic an amnesia, an entire episode, an entire period together, all gone. Right Tess?

T: Yes.

D: Who are you? Oh.

T: What's-her-name.

D: That's scary. Amnesia. To have people say, "Oh, yeah, I know Phil, I met him at so-and-so's," and I've never even seen them, I have no memory of the person or the place they're talking about.

I started remembering some of the terrible things that happened after Isa was born. Nancy went into a postpartum, her mental illness returned then. And do you know that I believed, honestly, that Nancy only got mentally ill the last few months that we were together, in '70? I had wiped out years of her wandering around with Isa for weeks, gone from my house for weeks, and terrible things like that. All wiped out. Really, you can understand why.

However, my point, what I'm trying to say, is that the taking of amphetamines at that point, I think, was masking why my memory was faulty and my behavior was erratic and my perceptions were disturbed. They were disturbed because of traumatic shock, and because of deeper mechanisms, like amnesia. But if I didn't take the dope, I would have to face it myself, and other people would have to face it, and it was easier to just pass it off in a simple way, "Well, he's spaced, he's spaced from the amphetamines."

W: Mainly Dex?

D: Yeah. And then down here, when I'd been several years off drugs, I was even worse spaced. Before Christopher was born, I was very frightened and nervous, I became even more spaced than ever and I wasn't taking anything. That was a shock.

W: You were hospitalized at one point, down here—I mean, other than for the shoulder?

D: No. Oh, well, just for high blood pressure. This year.

W: Do you do anything about that? Diet?

D: Yes, and I'm on medication for that. Isn't that funny? Can you imagine, you know . . . When I get spaced, I think, "Well, it's the amphetamines." And down here, years off it, and things got rough, and we ran out of money, and the baby was born and everything, and I got spaced on nothing. And it was obvious it never was the amphetamines, that I was spaced because I was scared; it was anxiety spacing me out, and causing amnesia and confusion and hysterical conversion things. It had nothing to do with drugs, nothing whatsoever. It's the damnedest thing. It mimicked, you see.

W: Yeah. Do you subscribe to the theory that the more aware we are of the nature of the world, both socially and whatever, emotionally, the more subject we are to this kind of experience?

D: You mean to the fears, or what?

W: The fears, yeah, the—

D: Traumas? Up to a point. Then . . . It's like a journey. Halfway through the journey there's a lot of trauma and a lot of tension. But if you pursue it all the way to the end, you come out where it's very, uh, um, peaceful. If you just keep on, if you don't bog down halfway. If you have the courage to continue on.

W: I mean, there's a real correlation between . . . I was

looking at a picture by Van Gogh in a museum, a month or two ago. And I just got hypnotized by . . . This one's somewhat of a self-portrait, he has those lines around the face—

D: Yeah.

W: Those lines in the air, I just felt like—his mind must have been so open to the world, in some way, so intense, and it's obvious there's such a great—at least some of the time—such a great deal of pain involved with that. There's just no question that the two things go together.

D: That's true. And I would have said a few months ago that that's where it ends—that is, in vulnerability, receptivity, and pain, trauma—but . . . I don't know, I've pushed it through to the point where I've reached, you know, I've touched a farther shore, where I've found peace and a sense of equilibrium and a sense of trust and, uh, my fear just—one day my fear went away and it has never come back. And I think I'm more receptive rather than less; it's not a case of blunting my receptivity.

But reaching that point, going from the Kierkegaard, you know, fear and trembling, to the thing beyond . . . When the peace that passes understanding came, it just came instantly, there was no process involved, I mean no stages, it just suddenly hit. One minute I was lying there at night as usual, unable to sleep, terrified of what lay ahead; I felt I'd be lucky if I lived till dawn, if they didn't get me in the night, they'd get me in the morning—and all of a sudden I woke up one day and I saw finite problems to deal with, and I dealt with them with alacrity and vigor, but no general thing; and then one day I realized I'd solved the finite problems, and I could trust the universe. I felt this tremendous faith, that it was helping me rather than screwing me up. It was watching very carefully to see what needs I had and doing everything it could to fulfill them.

In a kind of weird way, it was quite solicitous rather than either uninterested or . . . You've got three possibilities. It is either malicious; or it is completely uninterested and cold, in the sense of it doesn't care, you get ground up in the machinery and it doesn't notice you; or that it actually has a certain concern for you, and will do—make efforts, if you will only notice its proffering of help, but you must notice its proffering of help.

If it proffers it, you must be able to go halfway and receive it. And that's what I found, I had to watch where it proffered advice, assistance, and help—you know what I mean? The clues offered me, around me, in my world, were there, but not terribly blatant clues.

Phil had had a series of intense mystical/metaphysical/religious experiences in February and March of 1974, in retrospect probably the most powerful and profound experiences of his life. He talked to me about them, in a cautious way, when the tape recorder was off. I had difficulty understanding what he was telling me or what it was that had happened that was so important to him. This is apparent in my response to his last monologue, which I think was his first reference to the events of February/March in almost six hours of taped interviews. I went on with my train of thought. The significance of what Phil had just said, his acknowledgment of a total shift in the nature of his relationship with the universe, went right by me, unnoticed.

But the thoughts in Phil's mind seem to have a life of their own; and as you will see, the subject of what happened to him in February/March recurs in an unexpected form a few minutes later.

W: Would you agree that writing is a form of therapy?

D: Well, for me, it's more than that. It is a more vigorous, more active thing than most therapy. I think that's not a proper description of writing, in a way. It's a misleading thing to say, "Yes, it is a form of therapy," but certainly it would be more misleading to say, "No, it is not." I would say that it is a superior form of activity in terms of bringing about integration of the mind than therapy as such is.

But it should never—the goal of writing is not therapy. That's not its goal. So, it would be saying, "Is an automobile an attractive thing?" Well, attractiveness is not the prime purpose of an automobile. I mean, form follows function. The function of writing is not therapeutic. It may be as a spin-off that it will make you feel better.

W: What is the function of writing?

D: The function of writing—the function of writing depends on the person who's doing the writing. No general statement that I know of could be made.

W: In your case?

D: In my case . . . the function of writing is that I don't know what else to do with my time. I really, you know, I try other things, but I soon weary of them.

Like the function of watching TV is to watch TV; it's an end in itself. You don't do it to learn, like to learn about how people live. And the function of writing is to write.

W: Well, there's two states, right? There's the active one where you're actually writing the book; and there's also—after the book's completed you've got this completed object, and at that point some other relationship comes into existence, because you don't just throw away—

D: No, you sell it. For as much as you can get. You get very chintzy and mean, like Beethoven. He used to gyp people, he used to sell the same symphony to four orchestras at once.

W: [laughs] But you also care about it, on some level—

D: Well, I want it to be read. Is that what you mean? I want it to be read, because I want other people to know all that's there. It's important that they do it. But it's their problem to do it, I wouldn't make them do it, they've got to . . .

I put them on my trip. I wrote it—that was a hell of a lot of work—then they go on a kind of modified, easier version of my trip. And I figure, I got a lot out of it, they probably get something out of it, too. I don't think of it as entertainment for them, but a modified form of work for them, with a modified return.

W: Which will offer satisfactions, hopefully.

D: Yeah, I figure I got more out, though; I put more in, I got more out. Nobody can get as much out of a book of mine as I did. Because I'm deeper into it. I know more than they do. But that isn't really true, because people will point out things—especially academic people will point out things—that I don't know about my books, that I never noticed.

I read this article—did you read this article? *New Worlds for Old?* It's a book of criticism. . . .

W: Oh, yeah. But I don't think I read the part about you.

D: Oh, well, there's a thing about *Man in the High Castle,* and it explains that the pin on Juliana Frink's blouse is the symbol that holds everything together. You see. It represents that which holds everything together. And actually it holds her blouse together. But I didn't know that it held everything—the whole universe would collapse if that pin fell off her blouse.

W: There was a piece of jewelry in that book, but it was a different piece of jewelry. . . .

D: Yes, but, you see, he sees the relationship between the fact that the pin is jewelry. . . . Now, he's probably right; and I just never realized, you know, that—I emphasized at the end Juliana putting a pin on her blouse and holding her blouse together, that I'm carrying the jewelry thing . . . If the jewelry was a motif, a theme, a symbol before, why is it not, then, later? Why did suddenly jewelry cease to be jewelry and symbol, and just become a thing you hold your blouse together with? He's probably right and I'm wrong. I didn't sense that I was carrying . . . [From his tone of voice, Phil brought up the subject to mock the critic, and then as we spoke convinced himself that the critic was probably right.]

W: Yeah. It's, like, your personal experience. I mean, when I read *High Castle* the first time, I spaced out totally when I read, I guess, the part where Mr. Tagomi becomes very excited about—goes to another world and starts looking at this, whatever it was. . . .

D: Yeah, little jewelry squiggle.

W: And that, you know, just—it isn't necessarily an effect that a guy could repeat by reading it again. It's just something that happened to me at that moment.

D: Suffering succotash! Pardon me, I got off on what you were saying. I just . . . This whole experience of mine since March—of integration, and discovery of another world, and all that?—came about as a result of that girl coming to the door wearing a piece of handmade, extremely, marvelously modern jewelry with that fish symbol.

And I'm looking at it, and I say, "What is that you're wearing?" and pretty soon I'm in another universe, or . . . And the relationship between that and Tagomi doing that in the park with that thing—I never thought about it, but [he's getting truly excited, almost stuttering, clearly this is a new thought, new connection, and it's striking him very powerfully]—how else—what—what a—how—what a—what—what does this mean? This must mean something. This really must mean something.

W: It's like the *I Ching.*

D: The parallel is so obvious, now. I mean, I did what he did. I looked at that and I says—and I was spellbound, like Tagomi, I couldn't take my eyes off it. It was like, you know, it was like a little aperture, and it grew larger and larger over the subsequent days.

Now with Tagomi it was all at the moment. He walked around in the other world. And I looked at that jewelry she had on, and again, it was modern, handmade—it was gold, unique, never seen anything like it. And what do you know? Pretty soon I was, I literally was, in another universe. And I'm still in it.

Now here again, maybe I wrote more than I knew when I wrote the scene in *Man in the High Castle.* That sometimes these are focus points for . . . Like a pinhole camera! You make a pinhole and it lets in the entire world, through that pinhole.

I can't really ex— When you said this, about Tagomi doing that, I realized that you were talking about, although you derived this from a literary product, you were describing the way I would describe my experience of seeing an actual—

W: Right. Something just—happened.

D: Yeah. The only difference is, yours was in the book and mine was at the door.

W: Yeah, but—same thing. A piece of music, you know—

D: Yeah. [thoughtful] But with me it's so close to what happened with Tagomi. He perceived himself walking around in another San Francisco. He was in San Francisco, but it was a different San Francisco, and he sensed the difference.

And I've been walking around in Fullerton, but it's been a different Fullerton. And do you know, the funny thing is that for a while I speculated as to whether somehow I passed into an alternate present universe? Like in science-fiction stories. It did seem like that. It had more like that of an aspect than anything else. Now that I consider how Tagomi got into our world, which I guess that was, he got in through looking at a piece of jewelry. Suffering succotash. That's freaky, isn't it? And I looked at a piece of jewelry, years later, and then I noticed, in the subsequent days, that Fullerton was remarkably different. And I connected it with the jewelry. [deep breath] Gee. And I would never have known it if you hadn't been saying just what you said.

The incident of the girl with the fish necklace is fictionalized in chapter 7 of *Valis* and in chapter 14 of *Radio Free Albemuth.* And Phil describes it in detail in chapter 9 of *Philip K. Dick: The Last Testament,* by Gregg Rickman:

> It was a violent and incredible transformation of the land-

scape, of my perception of reality. It was triggered off by this Christian fish sign that I saw. . . . It stayed for one year, from February of '74 to February of '75, when I saw the world under the aspect of the Christian Apocalypse. It's what's called "stereographia." It literally means "to be covered over," or something that's hidden by being covered over, like hiding it under grass. It was like the stereographic covering of the world had been removed, and I was seeing the world as it really was.

CHAPTER NINE

"MOST CONSISTENTLY BRILLIANT"

Philip K. Dick is the most consistently brilliant science fiction writer in the world.

—John Brunner, 1966

Philip K. Dick takes greater risks than any American novelist now writing.

—Ursula K. Le Guin, 1982

Dick is quietly producing serious fiction in a popular form; there can be no greater praise.

—Michael Moorcock, 1966

In 1963, one science-fiction novel by Philip K. Dick was published. In 1964, four new Dick sf novels were published, followed by two in '65, three in '66, three in '67, one in '68, two in '69, and two in '70. That's eighteen novels in eight years. Thirteen of these books were paperback originals; the other five appeared in paperback not long after their hardcover publication. Most of Dick's nine earlier published novels were also reprinted during this period.

By the mid-1960s, in other words, there were a lot of Philip K. Dick novels available in the marketplace. If you got excited about one of his books, you could easily lay hands on and read a dozen others in the next few months. And that's exactly what would happen to many readers (and it's still happening). When I lived in Mendocino in 1969, I used to turn people on to Dick and then loan out his books to them in batches of three; they would inevitably come back a week later for three more. In 1985, in my role as editor of the Philip K. Dick Society newsletter, I frequently get letters from people who just a few months ago discovered Dick's work and have now read fifteen books and must obtain all the others. He tends to be read as he wrote: in large doses.

Readers immerse themselves in Philip K. Dick's world, and in many cases are never the same again. And this is not a local or limited phenomenon. Dick's reputation and popularity as a novelist grew faster and has gone farther in France, Japan, Germany, the United Kingdom, Spain, Australia, the Netherlands, Italy, and Sweden than in his native North America. He is a world author, and indeed for much of his life he received half or more of his annual income from sales outside the United States.

This is fortunate, because none of the twenty-seven Phil Dick novels published as of 1970 had earned him more than $2,500 for the initial sale. Most earned considerably less. So the money received when he finished a book didn't go very far, and of course this was a major factor in his writing so much.

It was not the only factor, however. The evidence is that there was seldom a time in Phil's adult life when he was not writing feverishly. Sometimes it was journal entries or mainstream novels rather than science fiction, in which case he didn't tend to get paid or praised for his efforts. But he wrote just the same, and he almost always wrote fast. It's true that a lot of the time he was on bennies or some kind of speed, but at any rate, that's how the man wrote: fast. Many times in his career, agents and book editors tried to slow him down; but the best they could ever do was force him to pretend he was going slower, make him put on a good act. The actual writing still came out like machine-gun fire.

> Dick is regarded by very many of his peers as the foremost science fiction writer of our time.
>
> —Thomas M. Disch, 1981

> Dick was probably the best science fiction writer of the past 35 years.
>
> —*Publishers Weekly,* 1985

> Sf's finest writer from 1956 to 1982.
>
> —John Clute, *Washington Post,* 1985

> "Important" is a rule from another game that I am not playing. I did not begin to read or to write sf for reasons dealing with importance. When I sat in high school geometry class secretly reading a copy of *Astounding* hidden within a textbook, I was not seeking importance. I was seeking, probably, intellectual excitement. Mental stimulation.
>
> —Philip K. Dick, 1980

> No other writer of his—our—generation had such a powerful intellectual presence.
>
> —Brian W. Aldiss, 1982

"Important" is a game Phil did try to play with his early mainstream work, and, though he denies it, a yardstick he often applied (sometimes with approval, often with condemnation) to his science fiction as well. But it seems very likely that his ability to put "importance" (whatever that meant to him, whatever it means to any of us) aside when he was actually writing science-fiction novels was the key to his enormous freedom of expression, and therefore his enormous success, when working in that form.

The Man in the High Castle was a turning point in Phil's career, not so much for its impact on other people's opinions of him as for its impact on his own self-assessment as a writer. Before *High Castle* he seems always to be reaching for something, and never certain whether he's achieved it or whether he's even capable of achieving it. After *High Castle* his writing is not necessarily better (sometimes it is, sometimes it isn't), but there's a freedom that wasn't there before, as if he's given himself permission, he's recognized and accepted that there is such a thing as a "Phil Dick novel," and it has a place in the universe, and if he just writes what comes out of him when he writes, he'll be doing his job in this lifetime.

Prior to writing *High Castle* he was holding back from science fiction in order to focus his energy on mainstream work. When he sat down to *High Castle,* he had no ambition left (temporarily); his only goal was to write, because it beat hell out of polishing jewelry under his wife's direction. And what came out of the typewriter was unexpected and marvelous.

And still he might have gone on—encouraged by the hardcover sale of *High Castle*—trying to gain acceptance at the court of publishable contemporary literature, but his next effort in that direction, *The First in Your Family (We Can Build You),* failed to find a publisher. And then on July 24, 1963, the Scott Meredith Literary Agency mailed him a huge package that must have had a stunning impact when it arrived at the Dick residence in Point Reyes a week later. It was all of the manuscripts of the mainstream novels that Phil's agent had been trying to sell for him for the last eight years or more, maybe a dozen in all. They were being returned as "unsalable." The long march was over. Years of hard work and ambition and hope had come to a complete dead end.

And then a month later, Labor Day weekend 1963, *The Man in the High Castle* won science fiction's highest award, the Hugo, for Best Novel of the Year. Phil had been rejected and thrown out in the cold and the door locked behind him on the one hand, and welcomed with open arms and hailed as a master on the other. The choice was no longer a difficult one. Science fiction couldn't offer much money or respectability, but it would allow him to write what he wanted. And it was home.

Phil completed four science-fiction novels in 1963, and an unbelievable six sf novels in '64. He needed the money, yes; but also he had discovered a form and a language all his own, and he babbled away in it as joyfully and tirelessly as any two-year-old.

For purposes of clarity, then, Philip K. Dick's career can be divided into three major periods (this is a variation on a system devised by Gregg Rickman with Phil's enthusiastic cooperation). The first starts in 1951 with the first stories he sold and ends in 1960 with *Humpty Dumpty in Oakland,* the last of the early mainstream novels. The second period begins with *The Man in the High Castle* in 1961 (these are dates of composition, not publication) and ends with *Flow My Tears, the Policeman Said,* in 1970. And the third period begins with his speech to the Vancouver science-fiction convention, "The Android and the Human," in 1972, and ends with *The Transmigration of Timothy Archer* in 1981.

The second period was the effusive one, when products of Phil's unrestrained imagination flowed out and filled the paperback racks around the world with stories of difficult marriages, drugs that alter the world forever and not necessarily for the better, dictators and industrial barons with soft hearts and huge insecurities, androids that masquerade as humans, suitcases that give psychiatric advice, and medical treatments that are supposed to increase intelligence but may actually be working in reverse.

It was also the period that produced the books that were most praised during his lifetime *(High Castle, The Three Stigmata of Palmer Eldritch, Martian Time-Slip, Ubik),* although there are as many different opinions as to which are his best books as there are Dick readers, and the consensus seems to be that his books overlap and have a cumulative impact that is very different from what can be found and pointed to in any individual Dick novel.

In terms of the progress of Dick's career during this period, it seemed outwardly static: He kept selling to the same markets, low-paying paperback publishers and one hard-cover house, Doubleday, that paid even less than some of the paperback houses (but did manage to swing some fair-size reprint sales for Phil toward the end of the decade). His foreign business steadily increased, as did the number of critics and fellow authors singing his praise, but it was all a kind of quiet progress, eclipsed by the melodrama of Phil's life, his marital problems and run-ins with the IRS (they seized his car) and so forth. At the end of the decade, he was writing another novel that he described as a potboiler (*Our Friends from Frolix 8,* actually an unambitious but very moving book) for an editor and publisher (Don Wollheim at Ace) he had sworn never to write for again. (Phil particularly resented Wollheim's criticism of his more experimental efforts.)

Writing a "quickie" for Wollheim for money was evidence to Phil that he had made no real progress in the marketplace, although the sale of *Flow My Tears* a year later, to Doubleday, was very fulfilling and did make him feel he'd reached a new level of acceptance as a creative and experimental novelist.

In truth, it was only at the very end that things got much better, although more money came in every year of the Seventies, mostly from foreign sales, reprints, and some movie deals. But after Phil wrote his self-proclaimed "masterpiece," *A Scanner Darkly,* in '73, he spent several years trying to find a publisher who would offer him more for it than the $2,500 Doubleday originally bought it for—and was unsuccessful. Bantam did buy *Valis* for big bucks, $12,000, in

'76; but once the finished manuscript came in, Bantam, who did only paperbacks, spent years trying to find a hardcover publisher for the book, and failed. In 1980 Phil finally sold a book—*The Divine Invasion*—to a hardcover publisher other than Doubleday, for the first time since 1961. Meanwhile science-fiction writers far less praised than he were enjoying hardcover best sellers and earning advances ten and even fifty times larger than the most he ever got for a book.

In 1975 *Flow My Tears* won the John W. Campbell Award, an odd but respected award given by the academic side of the science-fiction community. In 1977 Phil was guest of honor at the International Festival of Science Fiction in Metz, France. He was never guest of honor at the annual World Science Fiction Convention, perhaps because he was known to be a reluctant convention-goer at best. In 1974 when he was guest of honor at an important regional convention, he called in sick three months beforehand. He would frequently get sick or have other physical problems at times when he was scheduled to make public appearances.

Dick's "third period" is the least productive in terms of published output. From the outside it looks as though he finally slowed down and took more time with each individual book, which is true in a sense, and certainly the novels written during this period are more distinct from each other, have the feeling of being individually conceived projects that each received careful attention.

And indeed, more time was spent on most of these books—but not on the actual writing of them. Phil started working on the book that became *Radio Free Albemuth* early in 1974; it was originally planned as a short story for a collection Philip Jose Farmer wanted to do of stories written by characters from novels. The working title was "A Man for No Countries" (by Hawthorne Abendsen, of *High Castle*), and a handwritten note suggested it would be about " 'our' world (not quite) & what happened to me 11/17/71." The next evolution was apparently the plot Phil described to me during our interview. That was a book to be called *Valisystem A,* ostensibly a sequel to *High Castle;* the hero, Abendsen, sounds a lot like Phil after his family left and his house was broken into; and the entity, Valisystem, that contacts him sounds like whatever it was that interacted with Phil in March of '74.

In the summer of '76, Phil did write *Valisystem A* (published posthumously as *Radio Free Albemuth*). Clearly, he had worked on this book, gone through many evolutions of it, for more than two years. However, when he sat down to write, he did the actual writing in less than a month—in fact, incredibly, he wrote the novel once again as a "quickie" for Don Wollheim, now at DAW Books, because he needed the money! His agent submitted it to Bantam instead; Mark Hurst at Bantam bought it, but then persuaded Phil to rethink and rewrite the book. Two more years of procrastination followed.

In 1975 and for much of 1976 (before writing *Radio Free Albemuth*), Phil had called his work in progress *To Scare the Dead,* and said he had so far taken 100,000 (150,000; 200,000) words of notes for it. These notes were ostensibly research on the complex theological and historical background of the novel.

In fact, what Phil would do was read something in the *Britannica* or in a book, make a note about how it tied in to the projected plot of his book (in the summer of '75 he described that plot as "an ordinary businessman of modern day Los Angeles suddenly finds resurrected inside his own brain or mind the mind of an early Christian, an Essene of the Qumran Community of about 100 A.D."—again, a variation on what he believed had actually happened to him in March '74), and then proceed to speculate, speculate, speculate, about what had really happened and what it all meant.

He would talk to himself and make up theories and argue their merits and show how they tied in with other aspects of his experience and other research, on and on, page after page after page. These were his notes on the novel. Later he took to calling them his Exegesis. Evidently he started on it in 1974, probably soon after his experiences with Valis or God or whoever it was.

After Bantam bought and then put aside *Valisystem A,* Phil started corresponding with Mark Hurst about his plans for revising the novel, which he now began calling *Valis.* Phil's correspondence suggests that when he started writing *Valisystem A* as a quickie, his whole intention was to get it out of the way and go back to *To Scare the Dead.* But with thousands of dollars riding on his ability to redraft the Bantam manuscript, and with much of the material intended for *Dead* showing up in some form in *Valisystem A,* Phil put *Dead* aside and it was never heard from again.

Meanwhile Phil started writing to Mark about this whole new plot he was going to "laminate" on top of *Valisystem A,* involving another entity called "Zebra." There is a file of letters on this subject among Phil's papers—forty-three single-spaced pages, about 20,000 words, written between February 11 and March 17, 1977, all about how the new plot would work. Phil never actually did anything with it. He kept working on his notes.

Suddenly, in the fall of 1978, Phil responded with excitement to a letter from Russell Galen, an agent working at the Scott Meredith agency. Galen was not yet Phil's agent but had become fascinated with Dick's nonfiction pieces and interviews that he'd encountered in the agency files. He tried to interest a publisher in a collection of such pieces, and sent Phil a copy of the letter he wrote the publisher.

As Galen tells the story, Phil was apparently moved that someone out there, in fact someone working for his agent, believed in him so strongly; Phil told Galen that this reawakened his faith in himself, and in his ability to complete the novel he'd been blocked on for so long.

This is no doubt true, but it's also clear from what Phil has said about the incident that there was some actual clue in

Galen's letter that served as a disinhibiting agent, as it were, allowing Phil to see a new way to write about these experiences that had trapped him as a writer for so long—he didn't know how he could portray them in a novel (other than the rejected draft of *Valisystem A*) and he could not write about anything else until he had fulfilled his task of sharing this story with the world.

Shortly after receiving Galen's letter, Phil sat down at the typewriter, and less than a month later (late November 1978) was mailing his agent a manuscript entitled *Valis*—not at all a redrafting of *Valisystem A* but an entirely new novel, unlike anything Phil or anybody else had ever written before. The dedication read, "To Russell Galen, who showed me the right way."

I have a theory, by the way, that the "rejection" of the draft called *Valisystem A (Radio Free Albemuth)* was in fact a misunderstanding. I think Mark Hurst, as a fan of Phil's works, understandably imagined that Phil's technique was to take an idea, write a draft of a book, then sit down and write a second draft from the first, throwing in a whole lot more wild ideas, until finally he came up with that extraordinary thing called a "Phil Dick novel." So when Phil told Mark in his usual self-deprecating, self-protective way that the *Valisystem A* manuscript was "just a rough draft" (meaning he planned to type it again), Mark began excitedly chatting with Phil about all the things that could be added in the next go-round (playing editor), and Phil assumed that this meant the draft he'd written was unacceptable.

Phil was very nervous about sharing his metaphysical experiences with the world anyway, and had been shaken when Mark expressed a friendly concern that his friend and hero Phil had "gone religious on us." So Phil kept talking about how he would write a whole new draft (something he never actually did—his "drafts" seldom varied by more than five or ten percent from first to last, and amounted to a lot of fine tuning, a few inserted scenes, a few deletions); and

Mark would say that he loved the book but of course he was real excited to see how Phil would improve it. (And Phil was probably thinking, My God, I never got $12,000 for a book before, I'd better not blow this.)

The situation tied him in knots for years—he could rap about plot ideas endlessly, but he couldn't bear the thought of actually doing the kind of major rewrite he and Mark had discussed—until finally Russell Galen gave him, somewhat inadvertently, the clue and the courage to write a whole new book from the same premise, the book later published as *Valis.*

And the story still wasn't over. Phil called his next novel, completed in 1980, *Valis Regained.* (For a while *Valis* was referred to by Phil, after he wrote it, as *Valis Lost,* suggesting he was already thinking of it as part of a larger work.)

Valis Regained has none of the same characters as *Valis*—not even Valis itself is in the later book; it is written in a sharply different style, and the only similarity is a fascination with arcane theological speculation and a determination to transform such daunting material into an entertaining novel. Phil did establish an *ex post facto* link in later commentary that makes some sense: that *The Divine Invasion,* as *Valis Regained* was renamed on publication in '81, was in effect a science-fiction novel written by Horselover Fat, Phil's weird alter ego in *Valis.* Somehow this whole process, which had started with Philip Jose Farmer's idea of a story written by one of Dick's fictional characters, had come full circle.

Dick's last novel, which he proclaimed was killing him as he wrote it—he had prophesied his own death for at least two decades, and he finally got to be right—was a deliberately mainstream roman à clef about his old friend Episcopal bishop James Pike, who made headlines constantly during his outrageous tenure as archbishop of California, and who eventually died wandering around in the Dead Sea Desert looking for mushrooms or Christ or both.

The novel was called *The Transmigration of Timothy*

Archer. I call it deliberately mainstream because it was contracted for as a mainstream novel, unlike *A Scanner Darkly* (which was written as science fiction, even though it is only marginally sf and was published in hardcover as a mainstream book—for the ironic reason that it contained too many four-letter words to be included in Doubleday's sf line), and unlike *Valis* (which again is only science fiction by extension and courtesy, but which couldn't have been published if it hadn't been called sf, and barely got published even then).

Phil referred to *Transmigration* as "the third novel in the *Valis* trilogy" (which I suppose makes *Radio Free Albemuth* a precursor, like *The Hobbit*), because it again explores the religious/philosophical issues that so obsessed him—and indeed the three novels complement each other wonderfully. They explore related material in such different ways that it's amazing they're written by the same person—and yet none of them could have been written by anyone else.

So Phil spent 1974 to 1982 working on variations on the same theme—wrote four novels about it and conceived of plots for dozens of others. In total, Phil produced six novels during his third period, the last decade of his life—one of them a collaboration with Roger Zelazny that had its beginnings back in 1964—plus two other book-length works (a screenplay and a sort of epistolary novel made up of real letters he'd written). And right up to the end, though he spent plenty of time "getting ready" to write his books, the actual composition took place in a span of time seldom longer than a month or six weeks.

A final irony is the way it looks like Phil slowed down at least in his output during his third decade of professional writing. The second period was the floodtide—twenty novels published, as opposed to eight during the first period and eight during the third period. And yet, when you add Phil's Exegesis—over a million words of mostly handwritten notes, possibly closer to 2 million—Phil probably produced more wordage in his third period than ever before. The first period, too, is swollen by the twelve or more unpublished mainstream novels, most of them longer than his sf novels—and all those short stories. It ends up looking like he actually wrote less during his floodtide of productivity in the Sixties than he did in the Fifties or Seventies.

Basically, the man just loved to write. Intellectual excitement was the name of his game; he had a very excitable intellect. "Importance"—and he was and will continue to be an important writer to a lot of people—was only the icing on the cake.

It even scared him a little. If people choose their own deaths, he probably died because he was finally getting the kind of broad-based recognition he'd hoped for and feared all along.

CHAPTER TEN

SWALLOWED BY GOD

CONVERSATION, *November 2, 1974*

DICK: I was reading your early essays about me, and I noticed, as in *Actuel,* this word *paranoia* cropping up. [Phil and I had been looking at the September 1974 issue of *Actuel,* a French "underground press" magazine. It's a special issue on paranoia, and includes an interview with Phil Dick, who is called *"le grand paranoiaque de la science-fiction."*] It seems to be an obsession with you. How many writers have you defamed this way?

WILLIAMS: As paranoid?

D: Yes.

W: Only the ones who ask me if I'm going to call them paranoid or not.

D: I never asked you. . . . Well, *Actuel* has a lot to say about it.

W: Yeah, but you were going to say something. About paranoia.

D: Oh. Yeah. I used to be paranoid. Now, don't laugh when I say that. I mean it.

W: You were? In what way? Give me an example.

D: I thought my house was gonna be hit.

Now seriously. Are we talking seriously?

W: Yes. The tape recorder's on—

D: Then how come I've got a Life Saver in my mouth?

Okay. I used to believe the universe was basically hostile. And that I was misplaced in it, I was different from it. Cut off some other—cut off from—fashioned from some other universe and placed here, you see. So that it zigged when I zagged. And that it had singled me out only because there was something weird about me. It isn't so much that I blamed it, but I blamed myself. I didn't really groove with the universe.

Now, I had a lot of fears that the universe would discover just how different I was from it. My only suspicion about it was that it would find out the truth about me, and its reaction would be perfectly normal: It would get me. I didn't feel that it was malevolent, just perceptive. And there's nothing worse than a perceptive universe if there's something weird about you.

But this year I realized that that's not true. That the universe is perceptive, but it's friendly. And I don't know if you define the former as paranoia. There's different forms of paranoia. There's conspiracy paranoia—usually that's what they mean, you know, conspiracy paranoia . . . when people are sitting around, planning to get you, and they have malevolent motives, and there's something really great about you, and they don't want this to be allowed to go on, this greatness about you.

But I never felt that. I felt that I was a crumb. It was just a question—it was like, if I cheated in school, it was a question of time before they found out. So I always had this urge to confess to the universe my sins.

And I just don't feel that I'm different from the universe anymore. I never really felt it was malevolent. I just felt that—you know what I felt, Paul? I felt that the universe was so constructed that I could never really naturally follow the directions on anything and arrive easily and without effort at the right end. I think this is a learning thing, that the instructions that are easy for normal children are difficult for some children; they perceive a little differently, so that the ordinary instructions like "Color all the ducks yellow" somehow confuses some children for some perceptual reason.

I don't know if you would call this paranoia or just a sense of alienation, I think that there's lots of different kinds, and I just wonder about the term *paranoia,* because I tend to think of it more as a systemized view, very rigid systemized view, involving certain people or groups persecuting you rather consistently for malevolent reasons.

W: A lot like what happens to Jason Taverner [the protagonist of *Flow My Tears,* a TV star who suddenly becomes a nonperson; even his friends never heard of him, as though he were in the wrong world altogether].

D: Well, it's not me.

W: Well, why did you create that situation?

D: Um, that's just a plot thing. Also, he's found innocent at the end.

W: Yeah, well . . . You have paranoid plots. I mean, plots that are often motivated by paranoia. That isn't necessarily to say that you're a paranoid.

D: Well, you know, I think that where the linkage is, between what I had and clinical paranoia, is the sense of being watched. All paranoids feel they're being watched. And people can feel they're being watched—they call it paranoia sensitiva. It's a sense of body shame, or a sense of conspicuousness, and these are all just degrees.

If you're a hip dude and you show up by chance at a church social, you can feel—right?—paranoid, that you're being watched. And people thinking negative thoughts . . . And the thing that shows up in my books is that the characters are being watched all the time. That's Taverner: He's always being watched by the cops, they're always looking—

that's true, right? That does stem from my sense—I feel that I'm always in the public eye, that I have no privacy, there is no such thing as privacy.

I want to lay an idea on you, man. There are no privacies versus publixes any more.

W: There are no secrets.

D: There are no private lives. This is what Nixon found out. Course he engineered it himself, with the tapes. This is a most important aspect of modern life. As a science-fiction writer, dealing with the future, I want to speak to this. That one of the biggest transformations we have seen in human life in our society is the diminution of the sphere of the private. That we must reasonably now all regard the fact that there are no secrets and nothing is private. Everything is public.

Now, I used to think this was terrible, you know. I'll give you an example. One time this little kid came to the door and said, [high voice] "Can I have some papers?" Little girl. So I give her a lot, and she says, "I can't carry those." So I says, "I'll carry them for you. Where do you live?" "Up the street." So I'm carrying them, walking along with her, carrying all these *L.A.Times,* and I see a cop car parked. Just parked. And the cop sitting there watching.

W: And you think, Oh, my God.

D: Oh, my God.

W: They're gonna think I'm—

D: Yes.

W: —carrying these papers down the street for this little girl because—

D: I'm gonna molest her. And she says, "Carry them upstairs into my apartment." And I thought, Oh, my God, the end of my life has come. If I break and run, that'll do it, he'll come while I'm—

W: That's paranoid, Phil.

D: It certainly is. You better believe it is. And I carried them in, and I dropped them as fast as I could, and I walked back, and he sat there and he watched me as I walked back, you know. And I spoke to another little kid—they're all kids who collect newspapers—and as I passed his car, he started his motor and drove off. He was watching me. There was no doubt about it. 'Cause he waited till I had passed him, and then he started up and drove off. And he wanted me to know it. That's why he started up. He could have stayed there for eight years.

Now, I got home. And I was in an all-screwed-up state. My hair was all fizzled, you know, my eyes were all out of sorts. And I thought, Well, an end has to come to this some way. There has to be a way by which this is abolished. And then I got to thinking a lot of really heavy thoughts about it, you see. That the good side of this is, we are always under scrutiny, and that we should always regard it as such, and therefore we should never be hypocrites, we should never lie, you know, we should never be forked-tongue types, right? See, it's going to force us to be completely honest and consistent, because if we're not, we're screwed up. That's the good part of it. I mean, it's going to unify our public and private life.

But the bad part of it is that in a way we're at the mercy of other people, which is also part of a more densely populated society, you see what I mean? No isolation, no seclusion.

Now, I kept rethinking that situation. I should have walked over to that police car. And I should have said—

W: "Up yours, pig!"

D: No, no, that isn't right, no, you must be from out of town. I should have said, "Are you looking at me?" And he'd have just sat there. He wouldn't have said nothing. I'd say, "Well, I got something—" Well, no, I'd still be in the bucket, wouldn't I? I should have said, "You know who I am? I'm a famous per—" Well, no, that still would have got . . . Let's see. What would've been better than just slinking by the police car? Um. Walking up to him and showing him a photograph of my daughters? No, man, every act is self-incriminating, by virtue of the fact that one goes out of one's way.

W: It's obvious that you had a guilty mind.

D: You know what I thought of doing? Falling dead on the sidewalk. Just literally, like, arranging it so my heart stopped beating, I'd just fall dead. Now wouldn't that have made him stop suspecting me?

W: Yeah, he would have looked over and said, "Oh, well," and driven off.

D: Driven off a little sooner.

You know, suppose my heart—What am I saying? "Suppose my heart was absolutely pure"—it *was* absolutely pure. Talk long enough, Phil, and you will be in the bucket. Um . . . I should have said, "Officer, I want to commend you for watching over the lives of these little kids. With people like me around, you—" No, that ain't right either.

I think that for me it's hopeless; in situations of that kind, I will always feel— I should have said, "Officer, arrest that child!" I don't know, man. . . .

You know what? He was parked there to make people nervous; besides watching out for the kids, he was also parked there to make people nervous.

W: To make you turn over more newspapers.

D: No, I've never turned over any newspapers since then. In fact, I've never gone outside. He may still be there.

Now, about paranoia. The whole point of this was to explain that I wasn't paranoid.

W: Right.

D: I really feel that if I haven't convinced you so far, just go talk to that cop, about the guy that walked back on his hands and knees. . . .

I'll tell you, man. Paranoia, in some respects, I think, is a modern-day development of an ancient, archaic sense that animals still have—quarry-type animals—that they're being watched. Imagine you're a mole, walking across the field. You gotta have a sixth sense that something's overhead, cruising, like a hawk. Now, I say paranoia is an atavistic sense.

W: A what?

D: Atavistic. It's a lingering sense, that we had long ago, when we were—our ancestors were—very vulnerable to predators, and this sense tells them that they're being watched. And they're being watched probably by something that's going to get them.

This sense should be abolished by now. We shouldn't have it. But some people have a lingering sense, when they walk on a field, something's looking at 'em, see. And that's what paranoia is all about.

And often my characters have this feeling.

W: That they're being watched.

D: Yeah. But what really I've done is I have atavised their society. That although it's set in the future, in many ways they're living—there is a retrogressive quality in their lives, you know? They're living like our ancestors did. I mean, the hardware is in the future, the scenery's in the future, but the situations are really from the past.

Person at bay, you see, against the ring of hostile forces. It is a presocialized society, before communal and social living had developed where this instinct could diminish, disappear. So there's an element of the primitive in my characters, primitive in the sense of atavistic. They are isolates, pitted against everything that comes along.

But I just want to lecture you on being very careful about what you mean by the word *paranoia.* It's used a lot, as that article in *Harper's* says [a recent cover story about paranoia, which included a description of PKD's *Clans of the Alphane Moon*], it's used a lot as a kind of jargon word. Now I know you don't use it that way, but . . . It covers a multitude of crazinesses, and one of them is an atavistic thing, of a person who is not fully socialized, and therefore does not really know who is around him he can turn to. It's more of a primitive thing than anything else.

W: I think of paranoia as a heightened awareness of the connections between things.

D: That's true. The intuitive thing, that links stuff. You say, "This connects with that, and—"

W: And a, perhaps, imbalanced sense of the significance of those connections.

D: Correct. Jung said the same thing. It's a pattern. Aha! It all makes sense, it fits into place, right? Aha! Right? The significance of this detail, and everything has meaning. There's the spread of meaning throughout everything. Nothing has been overlooked. But everything in a way is equally regarded, you know, as fitting into a gestalt. It's overgestalting.

It assumes purpose, too—right?—where there's no purpose. Somebody bumps into you by accident—

W: And says, "Excuse me."

D: And you say—

W: "What did he mean by that?"

D: That's it, yeah. It's assuming motive when there is none. But you know, that article in *Harper's* is important, because it shows how this is a degenerated form of the old idea of a cosmology in which there are no accidents, and everything is part of God's plan, providence. We lose God and what are we left with? A network of connivance, without any benign center. And this assumption that people are motivated by hostility, that their motives are—that they're doing something bad when you can't understand what they're doing. I think there's more to it. I don't think any theory of paranoia really explains it, except the very classic clinical paranoia.

You know what I think? I think that these are complete failures in an attempt to understand one's environment as a true cosmology. And since one does not realize that unless one posits a basically benign force behind it, to start with . . . if one begins to construct a cosmology without it, it's very easy then to get into areas of malevolence. That we don't realize that at one time we posited to start with a benign superentity, right? God. And then assumed His plan from that, deduced the plan from His presence, and now we start seeing a plan. . . .

I'll give you an example of what I mean. You see a plan,

you see a pattern—one of the key words here is *pattern,* right?—you see a pattern of events, and if you have no transcendent view, no mystical view, no religious view, then the pattern must emanate from people. Where else can it come from, if that's all. . . ? And you start sensing a kind of a transcendent thing or mystical thing. Then you say, well, they didn't mean to do what they did; there's purpose in it, there's a pattern in it, the pattern is real, but they didn't intend it, they had no personal intentions, and it wasn't directed at me. They didn't mean it, and I'm not the victim, or target, of it. It's not aimed at me by them. It's a pattern, though.

I think we're getting a restricted view of actual patterns. And the restricted view says that people do things deliberately, in concert, aimed at me, where in truth there are patterns that emanate from beyond people. And they're certainly not directed at any one of us, you know; they're much broader, and they work through all of us.

But this requires a view that transcends social, human life, into a kind of mystical realm. Which could even be genetic forces, like the DNA forces, coding and so forth. I always think of the bug, saying, "Someone is trying to force me, someone is conspiring to make me weave a cocoon." And looks around at the other bugs. "I wonder which . . ." They're conspiring, you see. Without sensing a force outside of his own environment.

Please don't continually say I'm paranoid.

W: Why?

D: It makes me paranoid. . . . You know what I think? I think the thing is that paranoia must be pulled inside out. Absolutely inside out. It's not that it should be destroyed. I mean, that the solution to paranoia is to convince the person there is no pattern to the universe, that everything is chaotic, chance, and that people have no intentions. And that he is unimportant.

W: And it's all pointless.

D: Yeah. That's not the answer. To say, "You're unimportant, nobody cares about you, there is no meaning to anything, you'll die unnoticed. You have no purpose here on Earth. You're a negligible cog in a meaningless society. Now do you feel better?"

Turn it inside out, rather than just abolish it. That it's benign, and that it transcends our individualities and so on. The way I feel is that the universe itself is actually alive, and we're in it as part of it. And it is like a breathing creature, which explains the concept of the Atman, you know, the breath, pneuma, the breath of God . . . that the universe sort of breathes, we sense it, the movements back and forth, the systol—breathing in and out, whatever that's called, we sense its movement, like that.

It's not that individual objects are alive, it's the whole thing is an entity that is aware of itself, and we're part of it, and we're never outside of it.

And—and—and—you know, it's kind of—it's kind of—why don't you read that *Actuel?*

No, but you see this is the opposite of paranoia. I mean, it's the reverse of it. Another opposite is, there's no pattern, right? That's a way of saying opposite. But this is pulling it inside out, that everything is moving, changing, growing, developing, and that we move with it. We can never escape this movement, and its plans for us.

W: Try as we may.

D: Yeah. Like Jonah, trying to get away from the whale. "Trying to get away from the whale!" Trying to get away from God. I mean, it's a metaphor. He was swalled by God and the whale yelled at him and made God cough him up—I forget how that goes.

But you know, that we're part of it. And it's not that we're reified by that, it's just that—um—it's a pattern, and—why don't you read that *Actuel?*

* * *

I have tackled the *Actuel* with my schoolboy French, but nothing has been revealed. Michel Demuth's brief interview with Phil (1974) has the following subheads: "Le chaos," "L'acide," "Le suicide," "Les machines," "La société totalitaire," "La paranoia." Phil's comments on his suicide attempt in Canada, which led to his entering the heroin rehab place, bring me face-to-face with two ironies that I hadn't looked at closely before: that Phil had to pretend to be a junkie in order to get into X-Kalay, the inverse of his standard theme of the android pretending to be human; and that his purpose in entering X-Kalay was that he needed someplace where he could be *watched* twenty-four hours a day.

Under the heading "La paranoia," Phil says:

> Surprise is a sort of antidote to paranoia. To live in a way that you encounter a lot of surprises proves that you're not a paranoid. For the paranoid, there are no surprises; everything happens exactly as has predicted, everything finds a place in his system. For us, it is not possible to have a system. Perhaps all systems—that is to say all formulations, verbal, symbolic, semantic or otherwise, that claim to explain the universe by a universal hypothesis—are manifestations of paranoia. We must content ourselves with the mystery, the absurdity, the contradictions, the hostility, but also the generosity that our environment offers us. It's not much, but it's always better than the deadly, defeatist certainty of the paranoid.

CHAPTER ELEVEN

WHICH DREAMED IT?

Unlocking the front door of his house, he switched on the living room lights. And saw only rubble and ruin. Where his eleven-hundred-pound locked fireproof files had stood was a gaping blown-apart mass of papers, steel and the twisted edges of the asbestos sheets which had protected his precious manuscripts.

So came home science fiction novelist Philip K. Dick on that night in November, 1971, to a tract house already empty of wife and his little child Isa, not to mention the friends who had been staying with him. Stereo gone now, windows smashed in, doorlocks broken off—what did he think, viewing the empty spaces where his possessions had been five hours before?

Thank God, he thought. It was complete relief that filled him as he turned shakily and waved to the Yellow Cab to halt and head back, the cab which had brought him home after his car had mysteriously broken down on its trip to the grocery store at six p.m. that night. Relief, because even if he had nothing left in the world around him, he still had his mind intact.

> For six days police and friends had been telling him that it was only his paranoid imagination that his house was going to be hit—and hit hard, as in a commando attack during the Vietnam War. After all, didn't he write paranoid sf novels about people who believed they had invisible, powerful enemies, of a supernormal ability, about to destroy the hero? And which everybody else told the hero were merely in his mind?
>
> And, in his many novels and stories, didn't the hero prove suddenly to be right?

Looking through my papers, I recently found the above material. Phil had gone into the other room and written it, typed it, during my 1974 visit, after a conversation among him and Tessa and me about how the *Rolling Stone* profile might begin. Later I took this draft and rewrote it, with Phil's input, into the two paragraphs that begin this book.

The art of the novelist is to make his or her story real for the person who is reading it. Often (fortunately for fantastic novelists) this has less to do with the believability of the material than with the way the story is told. In the case of Philip K. Dick, he had the odd power of writing and speaking with complete conviction in the moment, even though he'd reported things differently a moment earlier and was well aware he'd probably see them another way tomorrow, or later in the chapter.

I don't mean he had the sociopath's power to imitate and project conviction. He was not a con man. He virtually always believed what he was saying, though his evidence might at times seem extremely flimsy to anyone else. He was a passionate seeker of the truth; and he found it, explored it, and expressed it, not at the end of the path, but at every possible station along the way.

I left Phil and Tessa's apartment on November 2, 1974, after hanging out with them for three very long, very intense days and nights. I took a commuter airline to Los Angeles

International Airport and flew up to San Francisco, on my way to Marin County to play investigative reporter.

This is what I wrote in the *Rolling Stone* profile about my own small search for the truth:

> In San Rafael I went to the offices of the local daily newspaper, the *Independent-Journal.* It took me two hours to find the item I wanted: one line, from the summary of residential burglaries reported by Marin and Sonoma law enforcement agencies the previous week. "Santa Venetia. Wednesday. Personal possessions valued at $600 taken Nov. 18 from the home of Philip Kindred Dick on Hacienda Way."
>
> There was one oddity about this item, perhaps meaningless—it was in the November 29th, 1971, paper, whereas all the other November 18th burglaries were reported in the summary printed a week earlier, November 22nd. Could this be corroboration of Phil's story about the police saying it never happened? Maybe this report was added to the following week's list, and back-dated, only after the police decided to list the break-in as a real event after all. Or maybe it was a simple clerical error. . . .
>
> I talked with two people who were around the house before and after the break-in. Both had seen the file cabinet and the rest of the house after the hit; both described the scene to me in some detail without contradicting any significant aspect of what Phil had told me. They both knew Phil, of course, but didn't know each other.
>
> Loren Cavit had been by the house a number of times; she invited Phil to speak to her high school class after reading a story of his in a textbook. Tom Schmidt, also in his young 20s, had lived in Phil's house in 1970, and was a frequent visitor the following year. When I called Tom and explained what I was doing, he started to answer some of my questions over the phone, then stopped.
>
> "This may sound funny, but there were a lot of strange things going on around that house, and, uh, this phone call would fit right in. . . ." I suggested he call Phil and check me out; he did, and the next day we talked over a cafeteria lunch at the Marin County Civic Center, scene of the courtroom

shoot-out that failed to free George Jackson and made a temporary fugitive of Angela Davis.

Tom thought Phil was "living in a fantasy world," but "he's entitled to go overboard in areas—it's part of his survival." What he saw of the house after the break-in made him believe that whoever it was, "they were looking for more than just something to sell." And he added that there had been at least two other burglaries of Phil's house, possibly inside jobs, probably motivated only by the cash value of the objects taken, prior to the November 17th break-in.

Loren Cavit said the file cabinet looked like it had been pried, but also said it looked burnt, and there were burn marks on the walls. And, "It must have been someone who knew when Phil would be out of the house, because he seldom was." I introduced her to a couple who also knew Phil, and all three agreed it was probably people who were in the house, around the scene, who did it.

The night after the break-in, Phil stayed at the house of another science-fiction writer, Avram Davidson. Avram said Phil professed himself to be "absolutely baffled" at who could have done it; at the same time he seemed "intrinsically undisturbed, marveling at the efficiency of the job."

I talked with people about the break-in not so much in hopes of "cracking the case" (I make an unconvincing California detective—unable to drive a car—taking notes I can't read later), but in hopes of seeing the damn thing from a different viewpoint. What I found was that the break-in seemed no less mysterious, but a lot less exciting, when seen through eyes other than Phil's. And I realized that it didn't really matter to me who broke into Philip Dick's house three years ago, and why. What I was really asking was a literary question, a theological question: How real is Phil Dick's sense of reality, and to what extent does it intersect with other ordinary people's, with my own?

My last stop, after saying goodbye to Tom Schmidt, was the second floor of the Civic Center, below the cafeteria, above the courthouse: the Marin County Sheriff's Department. I asked at the front desk for the police report on this particular burglary. They wouldn't show it to me, and sent me to someone else.

Each person told me he couldn't or wouldn't give me approval to check out the records, and shunted me to his superior when I persisted. Eventually a Captain Teague, the man in charge, agreed to help me out; he dug among the microfilm files himself for about ten minutes, then answered my questions while looking at the report under the magnifier. I couldn't see the report myself.

There was a metal cabinet, the police report said, that had been drilled or pried—the homeowner said it had been blown open but it looked to the reporting officer like it had been pried. A gun was taken. A stereo system was reported missing. The file indicated that there had been a previous burglary "not reported, but heard about indirectly." There was no information on further developments: "We didn't have any suspects." I asked about the guy supposedly arrested with the gun—Captain Teague said that would be a different case, not necessarily cross-referenced here.

That was all. I went downstairs and waited for my bus.

Where is reality? If what I found in Marin County is the sane and sober version—some stuff was taken, maybe people he knew did it—then I must say I prefer the crazy version, it's got a lot more life to it.

What is really going on? Phil Dick's reality intersects with mine in a lot of places, that is what attracts me to his books. He doesn't see things in dull probabilities. He sees all the sparkling—and terrifying—possibilities, the complex living and breathing and changing reality that other authors shy away from.

Here is a Phil Dick quote, out of context, from an unpublished collection of letters called *The Dark-Haired Girl:*

> Tessa and I started out with conflicting realities, found that when each of us reality-tested the other's, it collapsed. But now, instead of mutually destroying each other's realities, we are shaping a joint one between us. If two people dream the same dream, it ceases to be an illusion; the basic test that distinguishes reality from hallucination is the *consensus gentium,* that one other or several others see it too.
>
> This is the *idios kosmos,* the private dream, con-

> trasted to the shared dream of us all, the *koinos kosmos*. What is new in our time is that we are beginning to see the plastic, trembling quality of the *koinos kosmos*—which scares us, its insubstantiality—and the more-than-mere-vapor quality of the hallucination. Like sf, a third reality is formed halfway between.

> If two people dream the same dream, it ceases to be an illusion. Philip K. Dick's books and life are ultimately affirmative; they strengthen our sense of what is really real. They also feed our doubts about everything else.
>
> In the next decade or so, Phil's multiplex view of the world—his ability to see and deal with seven contradictory realities at once—may become a prerequisite to sane survival. More than one person has pointed out that reality—for all of us—is becoming more like a Phil Dick novel all the time.

Now as I complete this book it is 1985. I have become the temporary custodian of many thousands of pages of Philip K. Dick correspondence—I am the literary executor of his estate, supervising the posthumous publication of his previously unpublished writings—and as I read through the carbons of his letters, almost randomly, I'm finding out a lot of things I never knew or only half knew about Phil, his life, and his work.

But I can't say that I am any closer than ever to knowing what really happened on November 17, 1971. Nor did Phil, in the last eight years of his life, come up with any information I know of that totally confirmed or eliminated any of the various theories of the break-in we'd talked about in '74.

He did keep coming up with theories, of course. In November 1975, Phil wrote to Kent Bellows, whose full-color painting of Phil had just appeared in *Rolling Stone* facing the first page of my article:

> Listen, Kent, I want to tell you what you guys (Paul Williams, Greg [the *RS* art director], you) have done for me. You gave me a reflected self or identity and I suddenly believed I

was real. I am not shitting you. Something happened to me after I saw that color drawing of me you did. Back in 1970–72 in Marin County, that is exactly how I looked. I know the Man wanted me (for the law-infractions involved in my anti-war activity, which Paul didn't mention, because they are big raps). I expected the Man to hit me and wipe me out. So I did sit like you drew me, and peer around with that look. My shrink once simulated that look; it's the look, he said, of someone who believes (his term) that someone is going to get him. I told him about two weeks before the hit on my house that they were, and soon. He prescribed chlorpromazine.

But put more positively, you really changed me by depicting me in a real way. That picture *is* me. For it to be me, I must exist. You see, my friend, after the cops told me if I didn't move out of Marin County I'd get shot in the back or worse, and I flew to Canada as soon as the opportunity arranged itself, about a month later, I had already begun to keep such a low profile that my sense of existence was fading. I tried to become invisible, always.

. . . Then I returned from Canada, homesick. I tried to regain my identity. Obviously the old one had been scared into deep hiding. I only felt safe when I was with people, especially lots of people, like from the college here. I tried, but failed, to regain my identity, which, expressed another way, was, tried to lose the fear in me. I got remarried. I had a son. I made some bread, bought a car, all that, even a TV. But still my identity was a shadow, even to me. Only in public situations, like when I made a speech, was my existence ratified. Even when just my new wife and son were with me, I felt I didn't exist.

Then your picture came out. Frankly, Paul's article in itself, when I saw it before the printing, increased my fears. But here was some guy reconstructing me, the authentic me, just from snapshots. He—you—hadn't even seen me! You'd read some stuff of mine (I knew that) and I knew the limited material you had to work from . . . it was (I mean this) sort of holy magic, good magic. The creature who had been killed off in terms of identity up in Marin County a few years ago, still lived, still breathed, so in fact they hadn't killed him off. Your picture proved it. In essence, you reconstructed me and put life back into me.

From the moment I saw your picture, I was changed back to my old, real self. . . . You cured me of my identity-less sickness.

This is heavy stuff, but true. I've accomplished/done things I haven't done since before that thing you drew coming through my window first began to come through that window—1970; that's almost six years. No psychotherapy or psychiatry could or did help—I used to become paralyzed, literally, and then begin to shake, every time I saw a cop car. I know this doesn't make me look like much of a hero, but there was a lot of stuff Paul didn't mention; the cops actually smashed down my front door one night very late, and one time they came in and grabbed my girlfriend and held her in the police car until she was able to prove her age; they wouldn't even accept her birth certificate; "We have a tip on you," they told her. They had all kinds of tips—tips on drugs, on underage girls. The chief of the Marin County Youth Authority told me he had three five-year felony warrants he could exercise any time he felt like it, and he would if I ever "crossed the line and got into trouble again."

That man you drew, sitting in that chair, I thought they had in a very real way killed him. The real thing was, I found out recently from a producer who had researched me, was that I had been shot at because they (the authorities) thought I was a combination Tim Leary and Svengali "who was preaching dope and Communism to the kids there in the county." I wasn't, but I had kept a 14-year-old girl overnight because her parents had beaten her until she aborted. Next day I took her to the doctor, and he advised me to ask the authorities for custody, and, if necessary, to invoke the "Battered Child" Act. I had also, before keeping the girl all night at my house, phoned my attorney and he had agreed it was the right thing to do. We stayed up all night with a mutual friend.

The next day, the girl's parents and the police came. There were all those Che pictures on my walls, and posters from the Russian Revolution showing a clenched fist. Well, the next thing I knew, I wasn't seeing the Man to get custody of the girl; I was conferring with my attorney to keep from being charged on several felony counts. That's where that remark by the police sergeant, "Marin County doesn't want any crusaders," comes in; it was accompanied by, "Those kids need discipline, not understanding." But until the producer told me very recently that the inside story was about my giving classes, secretly, to the kids, on Communism, drugs and sex, I didn't know.

"Are you going to start up operations again?" one policeman asked me, after the hit. I didn't know what he meant by "operations," so I said no (notice the crumbling of pride and identity already at that moment—saying "no" without even knowing what "operations" means). I really seemed a menace to the establishment. Tim Leary was indeed an admirer of my work and had phoned me to say so, and of course I told everyone that. And I was in the drug subculture. And most of the people who came to my house were a lot younger than me; Paul had in his original draft that I had turned to friendship with teenagers because of the deaths of two close friends my own age, Jim Pike and Tony Boucher, and this is somewhat true, but more true was the fact that no one my age (45) is worth talking to. I still can't talk to them. "Nice weather we're having." "Yeah, but the smog count—", etc. My wife is only 21; I met her when she was 18 and started living with her then.

My relationship with Phil gets stranger and stranger. I often feel when I'm putting together collections of his writings that he's collaborating with me, which of course he is, but I mean in a very active and immediate way. For example, I never saw the letter I just quoted above till a few days ago. There is such a vast amount of material in the Dick papers that if I were to become familiar with it all before writing this book, say, it would be delayed at least ten years. And that's assuming I could actually find the energy to read it all, and not lose my mind in the process. So it feels, you see, as though Phil or the universe pushed that letter into my path, maybe even wrote it on the spot, in order to add a few more powerful twists to our old bit about the theories of the break-in, now that I'm down to the last chapter, not to mention twists on the themes of amnesia and paranoia and Phil's nervous breakdowns and . . .

These surprises (I never heard those stories in the letter before, although Phil implies that I did) and complications and disturbing revelations and alternate viewpoints are awfully reminiscent of the last chapters of a Philip K. Dick novel. "You gave me a reflected self or identity and I suddenly believed I was real." Very clever, Phil. Now where do we go from here?

Flow My Tears, the Policeman Said opened in Boston last month as a play, a theater piece, by one of the most respected, craziest, most creative avant-garde theater groups in the world, Mabou Mines. A New York production follows. Phil gets top billing in the playbill—clearly the intention is that this be a Philip K. Dick creation, not somebody else's creation "based on" his ideas. Kent Bellows's portrait of Phil from *Rolling Stone* is on the cover of the program. Bhob Stewart (the very same who read to me from *Time Out of Joint* so many years ago) has been sending me clippings and transcripts of all the press coverage in Boston—there's been a tremendous amount. Four other Dick novels have been the basis for avant-garde plays in the last two years. And a young composer named Todd Machover has been commissioned by the Georges Pompidou Centre in Paris to write and produce an opera based on *Valis.*

This sort of thing would have meant more to Phil than Hollywood movies and TV adaptations, although it looks as though there will be plenty of those as well. And five new, previously unpublished books by Philip K. Dick were published in hardcover(!) in 1985, and many more are on the way, including a complete short stories, in two massive volumes. If that sounds too respectable, check out the number of punk and avant-garde rock musicians who credit Phil with helping to inspire their work.

And as I write, two different magazines in California are preparing stories that call attention to Phil primarily as the author of the Exegesis. I would have guessed it would have been ten more years before that would start attracting public interest. The Philip K. Dick Society newsletter is up to its eighth issue, has an international circulation of more than 600, and is growing steadily. Dozens of books about Phil are out or in the planning stages, around the world. I even found myself, one evening last winter, cutting the signatures out of Phil's old canceled checks (some of them pre-'71, that somehow survived the break-in) so they can be embossed into special limited editions of his books selling for as much as $180. I guess when your friends get gainful employment cutting the signatures out of your old checks, you've made it.

If Phil were alive, all this activity would delight him—and fill him with unspeakable dread. He had fun playing hardball with the *Blade Runner* people—they wanted him to write a novelization of their script for a tie-in book and to suppress *Do Androids Dream of Electric Sheep?* and he told them to take their $400,000 offer and stuff it, and settled for $25,000 and a proper tie-in reprinting of *Androids* instead. But the stress was enormous. And the anticipation of what it would be like if the movie were a smash hit—as he later came to believe it deserved to be, after he read the revised script—filled him with fear. I think he sensed that this could be an even more demanding public situation than being guest of honor at a science-fiction convention.

There is no end to the stories I could tell about Phil Dick. Sometimes I think he invented me to tell these stories, along with Gregg Rickman and Patricia Warrick and his other biographers. And I point to all the non-PKD-related creative work in my life, to reassure myself that I do after all still have an identity of my own, and then I think that's just how he would have invented me, to be this guy who started a rock magazine and who helped publish the first book edition of *The International Bill of Human Rights.* All that stuff helps make me a more complex and believable invention.

There is no end to the stories I could tell about Phil Dick. The more I learn about the man and his life and work, the more questions I have, and the more there is to know. Every piece fit into the puzzle somehow expands the puzzle, creating new and larger openings to be filled. This is not a progression toward order. I mean, this is not a simple progression toward order. It is a constantly expanding exploration of the complexity of order and of the beauty of this unstable, uncertain, but always meaningful universe in which we find ourselves. The deeper I go into Phil's *idios kosmos,* the more I discover about my own *idios kosmos*—and the more powerfully I sense the presence of a *koinos kosmos* more compelling and more real than anything I had previously accepted as reality.

How real is Phil Dick's sense of reality? Real enough to survive him, to live on and change and grow. And, yes, it intersects with ordinary people's, but in unusual, extraordinary ways. Phil's sense of reality doesn't conform to existing literary or philosophical or even commonsense standards. It is strong enough to stand alone, and new standards are forming as a result.

This is in a real sense a defeat of death, as in the ambiguous and haunting last chapter of Phil's last book, *The Transmigration of Timothy Archer.* Timothy Archer, like the Wub in Phil's first published story, refuses to die in the ordinary sense; or rather, he welcomes death and then goes right on with what he was saying.

If the past lives on in the present, clearly the present lives on in the future. Glen Runciter in *Ubik* keeps sending messages to his employees even though he died at the beginning of the novel. And these don't seem to be messages from the past, but very much part of and related to the present. Eventually the possibility is raised that maybe all of us are dead and he's the one that's alive. Maybe the past is bigger and more real than what we experience as the present. The *koinos kosmos* in *Ubik* is collapsing into its own past, so that a 1992 air taxi becomes a 1939 LaSalle automobile. Reality is shedding its costumes and reverting to earlier forms.

Phil wrote *Ubik* twice: once in 1966, and then again in 1974, as a screenplay. I wrote this profile twice: as a magazine piece in 1974, as a book in 1985. Now I'm finished and I have to stop, and I'm afraid that my friend will stop talking. I understand why Phil had such trouble with endings and why, as Ursula K. Le Guin said, all his writings run together into one enormous novel. This book is part of that novel, and I, as author, am a character in it. I'm going to leave you now with this quote from Phil's *Ubik* screenplay:

> Perhaps this verifies an ancient philosophy: Plato's ideal objects, the universals which in each class are real. Prior forms must carry on an invisible, residual life in every object. The past is latent, submerged, but still here, capable of rising to the surface once the later printing, through some unfortunate accident, vanishes. The man contains—not the boy—but earlier men. But didn't Plato think that something survived the decay and decline of forms? Something inside, not able to decay? The body ending, like Wendy did . . . and the soul: out of its nest the bird, flown elsewhere. To be reborn again, the Tibetan Book of the Dead says. It really is true. Christ, I hope so. Because then we can all meet again. As in Winnie-the-Pooh, in another part of the forest. . . .

APPENDIX

NOVELS BY PHILIP K. DICK IN CHRONOLOGICAL ORDER OF COMPOSITION

1. *Return to Lilliput* (not extant; referred to by PKD in Boonstra interview, 1981, as his first novel, started when he was thirteen [1942]. There are probably other early novels of which neither manuscript nor name survive.)

2. *The Earthshaker* (1948–50; the first few chapters and an outline are in the PKD papers. This could be the "long ago straight novel" that later served as a basis for *Dr. Bloodmoney,* per PKD letter to S. Miesel, 9/8/70.)

3. *Voices from the Street* (date unknown, sequence uncertain—possibly the first of the extant novel manuscripts—circa 1952–53; 547 pages; in 1974 PKD guessed its date as 1954 and said it was perhaps the earliest of the existing mainstream novels.)

4. *The Cosmic Puppets* (original manuscript title *A Glass of Darkness;* received at Scott Meredith Literary Agency 8/19/53; science fiction; published in magazine in 1956; published in slightly altered/expanded form as a book in 1957.)

5. *Gather Yourselves Together* (date unknown, sequence uncertain; mainstream; 481 pages.)

6. *Solar Lottery* (original manuscript title *Quizmaster Take All;* published in the United Kingdom in slightly variant

form—due to editorial changes demanded by U.K. publisher—as *World of Chance;* received by SMLA 3/23/54; science fiction; PKD's first published novel, published by Ace, May 1955.)

7. *The World Jones Made* (original manuscript title *Womb for Another;* received by SMLA 12/13/54; science fiction; published 1956.)

8. *Eye in the Sky* (original manuscript title *With Opened Mind;* received by SMLA 2/15/55; science fiction; published 1957.)

9. *Mary and the Giant* (date uncertain, sequence uncertain; letter from publisher discussing it, in PKD papers, is dated 6/2/55; mainstream; 315 pages; probably written in 1954 or early '55. PKD remembered this in 1974 as the first "experimental" novel of his that came close to selling, and there is evidence in letters from publishers that Crown came very close to publishing it [1956] and Julian Messner thought enough of it that the editor wrote Phil a four-page letter about possible revisions [1955].)

10. *The Man Who Japed* (received by SMLA 10/17/55; science fiction; published 1956, after *Jones*.)

11. *A Time for George Stavros* (SMLA started marketing circa 1/56; mainstream; manuscript no longer extant—may have been destroyed by PKD when he wrote *Humpty Dumpty,* which is apparently a rewrite or recasting of *Stavros*.)

12. *Pilgrim on the Hill* (received by SMLA 11/8/56; mainstream; manuscript no longer extant; it was returned to PKD by SMLA with his other unsold mainstream novels in a large package 7/24/63, but did not end up at Cal State, Fullerton, in 1972—lost or destroyed somewhere along the way.)

13. *The Broken Bubble of Thisbe Holt* (received by SMLA 11/13/56; mainstream; 350 pages. There is no explanation of why this and *Pilgrim* arrived so close together at SMLA—possibly one or both are rewritten from earlier drafts previously circulated to publishers. In 1974 PKD characterized *Thisbe* as "excellent.")

14. *Puttering About in a Small Land* (received by SMLA 5/15/57; mainstream; published 1985. In 1974 PKD characterized *Confessions* as "best" and *Puttering* as "second best" of his mainstream novels.)

15. *Nicholas and the Higs* (received by SMLA 1/3/58 at 128,000 words; revised manuscript received by SMLA 4/30/58 at 75,000 words; mainstream with sf/fantasy elements, apparently; manuscript no longer extant, although returned to PKD 7/24/63.)

16. *Time out of Joint* (original manuscript title *Biography in Time;* received by SMLA 4/7/58; sold to Lippincott, PKD's first U.S. hardcover sale; published 1959; science fiction, although published as "a novel of menace.")

17. *In Milton Lumky Territory* (received by SMLA 10/8/58; mainstream; published 1985.)

18. *Dr. Futurity* (received by SMLA 7/28/59; expanded, rewritten version of "Time Pawn," novelette originally received by SMLA 6/5/53; science fiction; published 1960.)

19. *Confessions of a Crap Artist* (date of receipt uncertain, but no later than 9/59; probably completed summer 1959; mainstream; came very close to publication, especially with Knopf, but PKD was unwilling or unable to attempt a rewrite in response to their suggestions; manuscript was submitted to publishers under the pseudonym Jack Isidore; published 1975, the first of the mainstream novels to be published.)

20. *Vulcan's Hammer* (revised manuscript received by SMLA 2/16/60; revised, expanded version of novelette originally received by SMLA 4/16/54 or possibly 4/16/53; science fiction; published 1960.)

21. *The Man Whose Teeth Were All Exactly Alike* (received by SMLA 5/10/60; mainstream; published 1984.)

22. *Humpty Dumpty in Oakland* (received by SMLA circa Oct.–Nov. 1960; mainstream; 283 pages; apparently partially based on *George Stavros*.)

23. *The Man in the High Castle* (received by SMLA 11/29/61; science fiction; published 1962; Hugo Award, Best Science Fiction Novel of the Year, 1963.)

24. *We Can Build You* (original manuscript title *The First in Your Family;* serialized as *A. Lincoln, Simulacrum;* received by SMLA 10/4/62; hybrid mainstream/sf; serialized 1969; published as a book 1972.)

25. *Martian Time-Slip* (original manuscript title *Goodmember Arnie Kott of Mars;* serialized as *All We Marsmen;* received by SMLA 10/31/62; science fiction; published 1964.)

26. *Dr. Bloodmoney, or How We Got Along after the Bomb* (original manuscript title *In Earth's Diurnal Course,* received by SMLA 2/11/63; science fiction, based on an earlier PKD mainstream novel according to PKD; published 1965.)

27. *The Game-Players of Titan* (received by SMLA 6/4/63; science fiction; published 1963.)

28. *The Simulacra* (original manuscript title *The First Lady of Earth;* received by SMLA 8/28/63; science fiction; published 1964.)

29. *Now Wait for Last Year* (received by SMLA 12/4/63; science fiction; revised at least once before publication in 1966.)

30. *Clans of the Alphane Moon* (received by SMLA 1/16/64; science fiction; published 1964.)

31. *The Crack in Space* (original manuscript title *Cantata 140,* first half received by SMLA 9/9/63 and sold in revised form as short novel to magazine; completion received by SMLA 3/17/64; science fiction; published 1966.)

32. *The Three Stigmata of Palmer Eldritch* (received by SMLA 3/18/64; science fiction; published 1965—the first of eight PKD novels published in hardcover by Doubleday.)

33. *The Zap Gun* (outline received by SMLA 12/5/63; completed manuscript received by SMLA 4/15/64; science fiction; original manuscript in PKD papers is longer than published version; published 1967.)

34. *The Penultimate Truth* (original manuscript title *In the Mold of Yancy;* outline received by SMLA 3/18/64; completed manuscript apparently received by SMLA 5/12/64; science fiction; published 1964.)

35. *The Unteleported Man* (first part apparently received by SMLA 8/26/64, published in magazine, ultimately published as book in 1966; second part received by SMLA 5/5/65, unpublished until new revised edition, 1983; another, further revised edition was published in the United Kingdom in 1984 under the title *Lies, Inc.;* science fiction.)

36. *Counter-Clock World* (original manuscript titles *The Dead Are Young* and *The Dead Grow Young,* date of composition and receipt uncertain—I estimate late 1965; science fiction; published 1967.)

37. *The Ganymede Takeover* (by Philip K. Dick and Ray Nelson; original manuscript title *The Stones Rejected;* outline received by SMLA 11/13/64; date of completion uncertain—possibly 8/16/66, which is date of sale; science fiction; published 1967.)

38. *Do Androids Dream of Electric Sheep?* (original manuscript title *The Electric Toad,* alternate titles on later manuscript include *Do Androids Dream?, The Electric Sheep,* and *The Killers Are Among Us! Cried Rick Deckard to the Special Man;* received by SMLA 6/20/66; science fiction; published 1968; has also been published under the title *Blade Runner.)*

39. *The Glimmung of Plowman's Planet* (received by SMLA 12/7/66; children's science-fiction novel; 98 pages.)

40. *Ubik* (original manuscript title *Death of an Anti-Watcher,* received by SMLA 12/7/66; science fiction; published 1969.)

41. *Galactic Pot-Healer* (PKD in correspondence indicates publisher received manuscript in mid-March 1968; science fiction; published 1969.)

42. *A Maze of Death* (original manuscript title *The Name of the Game Is Death;* outline received by SMLA 5/4/67; finished manuscript received 10/31/68; science fiction; published 1970.)

43. *Our Friends from Frolix 8* (portion and outline received by SMLA 11/6/68, completed manuscript received by SMLA 7/2/69; science fiction; published 1970.)

44. *Flow My Tears, the Policeman Said* (complete draft finished 8/7/70; subsequently revised; science fiction; published 1974.)

45. *The Dark-Haired Girl* (received by SMLA 11/28/72; letters by PKD assembled by PKD as a book manuscript; not a novel but presented as a narrative; 126 pages.)

46. *A Scanner Darkly* (first draft completed 4/14/73; revised manuscript received by SMLA 8/29/75; mainstream with science-fiction elements; published 1977.)

47. *Ubik* screenplay (completed mid-October 1974, based on PKD's novel *Ubik;* included here as a major narrative work; published 1985.)

48. *Deus Irae* (by Philip K. Dick and Roger Zelazny; original working title *The Kneeling Legless Man;* outline received by SMLA 3/27/64; finished manuscript received by SMLA circa 8/17/75; science fiction; published 1976.)

49. *Radio Free Albemuth* (original manuscript title *Valisystem A;* received by SMLA 8/19/76; mainstream with science-fiction elements; originally purchased as a rough draft; after several years of failing to revise it, PKD wrote *Valis* instead; published in its original form, 1985.)

50. *Valis* (original working title *To Scare the Dead;* received by SMLA 12/7/78; mainstream with science-fiction elements; published 1981.)

51. *The Divine Invasion* (original manuscript title *Valis Regained;* outline received by SMLA 3/14/80; manuscript completed May/June 1980; science fiction; published 1981.)

52. *The Transmigration of Timothy Archer* (original manuscript title *Bishop Timothy Archer;* outline received by SMLA 4/15/81; manuscript completed 5/13/81; mainstream; published 1982; PKD's last novel—another one, *The Owl in Daylight,* was contracted for but never written.)

BOOKS BY PAUL WILLIAMS:

Practical philosophy:

Das Energi
Remember Your Essence
Fear of Truth (*Energi Inscriptions*)
Waking Up Together
The Book of Houses (with astrologer Robert Cole)
Coming
Nation of Lawyers
Common Sense
How to Become Fabulously Wealthy at Home in 30 Minutes

Hippie memoirs:

Time Between
Apple Bay or Life on the Planet
Heart of Gold

Collections:

Pushing Upward
Right to Pass and Other True Stories

Music:

Performing Artist, The Music of Bob Dylan, Volumes I & II
Brian Wilson & the Beach Boys—How Deep Is the Ocean?
Neil Young—Love to Burn
Rock and Roll: The 100 Best Singles
Watching the River Flow: Observations on Bob Dylan's Art-in-Progress 1966-1995
The Map—Rediscovering Rock and Roll
Outlaw Blues
Back to the Miracle Factory

Other arts:

The 20th Century's Greatest Hits
Only Apparently Real: The World of Philip K. Dick

Edited by Paul Williams:

The International Bill of Human Rights
The Complete Stories of Theodore Sturgeon
(magazines: *Crawdaddy! The PKD Society Newsletter*)

www.ingramcontent.com/pod-product-compliance
Ingram Content Group UK Ltd.
Pitfield, Milton Keynes, MK11 3LW, UK
UKHW041838190726
13854UKWH00002B/604

9 780934 558310